Debrah,
Blessing as you
venture into ministry
Don Murray

Celebrating Eve
Christianity as a Pathway to Wholeness

Don Murray

Glen Margaret Publishing

Other books by the author
  For Unbelieving Christians
  From Pisces to Aquarius

edited by Jim Taylor
layout and design by Brenda Conroy and Richard Rogers
printed in Canada

Cover Art: *Coding of a new covenant in a time of crisis*.
Paige Prichard Kennedy. R.R. # 1, Scotsburn, N.S.,
B0K 1R0. Phone (902) 351-2071.
E-mail <pairlie@north.nsis.com>

Songs: Emily Kierstead. *Eve*, *Lament*, and *Holy of Holies* from her CD *Womanspirit*. *It's Time* is unrecorded. R.R.# 2, Brookfield, N.S., B0N 1C0. Phone (902) 673-2909.
E-mail <emilydon@north.nsis.com>

Author's photo: Jonathan Kierstead

National Library of Canada Cataloguing in Publication Data

Murray, Don, 1933
        Celebrating Eve

Includes bibliographical references.
ISBN 0-920427-50-2

        1. Apologetics. I. Title.

BT1103.M87 2001   239   C2001-900295-5

To

Emily,
my partner and soul mate,
who delights in the Eros of life

Tatamagouche Centre (A.C.T.C.),
the place and the people who have midwifed
and nourished my soul's journey.

Jean Houston,
who opened my being to a wider and deeper vision

Contents

Jesus

Humanity

Foreword

What a pleasure! I read about half of your manuscript, but then felt it really deserved more time — section by section, with more reflection on each.

It is powerful, challenging, exciting, and well-written. I like the way you keep your personal voice in it. It feels like a conversation with you. I really like the sections on patriarchy and gender (indeed, that theme really flows through all of it).

You have very systematically worked through many of the theological questions I am just on the verge of considering. As someone once said of good poetry — it is thoughts overheard. I have the same sense that your work articulates some of my deeper thinking, feeling, searching and really helps me to move forward.

Your clarity, for example, about the "Ultimate Mystery" which is pure Eros, with "Yahweh" being the Hebrew "take" on this, is very helpful to me. It gives a great basis to think of inter-faith dialogue in a very constructive way. Beneath all human search for meaning is the great Mystery, the yearning love searching for relationship. Each religious tradition gives us its deepest truths through the culturally-constructed gods and goddesses which embody their best understanding of the greater mystery.

I also really relate to the piece where you talk of all of us yearning to have more time for meditation, reflection, etc., but the day-to-day life intervenes, yet in the end it is in the busy, boring, stuff that we are challenged. Indeed, this "real world" is the fertile ground from which grows our own transformation.

I find the last section on "Humanity" really brilliant. I think it brings the whole book together very well and really challenges and stretches my thinking. I have been thinking of this section many times since reading it. Thanks for doing it! The universe is the better for it.

by Dr. Wilfred Bean
(Former professor at the Coady International Institute, St. Francis Xavier University; now Program Director at Tatamagouche Centre)

Preface

We live in dangerous and exciting times. Powerful forces awaken us to new levels of awareness, yet the survival of humanity is not assured. Whatever the exact date of the arrival of the new millennium, it stands as a symbol of major transformations taking place throughout the earth. If we cannot become a world community of justice and mutual respect, our individualism and nationalism will destroy us. Western civilization, having evolved the technology and competence to create the "global village," is depleting the world's resources at a rate which cannot be continued. If we are to survive and thrive the rising human consciousness must soon reach "critical mass."

This book is for the searchers and seekers, those who are keenly aware of the bankruptcy of western culture and who hunger for depth and connection. You may sense that Christianity contains truth and power but have not found it within the church. Many have left. Others hang in, hoping. Some are returning to search again, and discovering that here and there light shines.

But, for the most part, traditional western Christianity is slipping into the pages of history. Clothed in the language and thought forms of another age, it has become an empty shell with little power to grasp our hearts, minds and souls and give meaning and direction to our lives. As Bishop John Shelby Spong says, it must "change or die."

The forces of change, of course, work within Christianity as they do everywhere. Having been moulded and shaped by the Christian tradition, my goal is to help you meet Christianity "again for the first time"[1]; to look at Christianity, and its Scriptures, through the eyes of today's world and find again its wisdom and power. I honour and value the ages of Christianity which have brought us to this time. Now we must clothe this religious faith in the garment of this age.

This book, a collection of Think Pieces, is my word in the conversation. I see the Judeo-Christian scriptures as a mythology of humanity's growth toward wholeness — not a new idea, but one being rediscovered and presented in modern dress. From the first tentative steps of Eve in the Genesis account of the Garden of Eden, to the final consummation of the New Jerusalem in the closing chapters of Revelation, I present the Bible as the story of a people learning what it means to become fully human. Since Eve is the mythic figure who took that first bold step, I write in celebration of Eve.

Biblical quotes are from the New Revised Standard Version (NRSV) unless otherwise indicated.

Chapter subheadings refer to the biblical material being considered, or the general theme being presented.

Don Murray

Acknowledgements

I gratefully acknowledge all those who made this writing possible. I know clearly that there is no such thing as a new thought. We simply weave the thinking of others in a slightly different pattern.

To all those past and present who have come to me through books, especially the Bible, I say "Thank you." Some appear in the Bibliography. My thanks go to all who have helped and encouraged the latest evolution in my thinking. Attending Jean Houston's Mystery School was a wild and wonderful experience that greatly helped in opening me to mythology, the feminine, spirituality, Jungian psychology, modern physics, and sacred traditions both ancient and modern. Michael Dwinell pushed, pulled, and challenged me through an important time of personal growing. Eldon Hay has been a constant friend, challenging and affirming my journey. Freda McCormick has forced me to clarify my thinking in many a discussion.

Integrating these things around the Christian tradition is my continuing work. Many people, and especially those of Tatamagouche Centre (an adult education centre of The United Church of Canada), have nourished and supported my journey. The Centre staff, notably Kathryn Anderson and Bill Leslie; the people in the many events in which I participated; the continuing groups to which I belong: The Weavers; The Men; The Intuition Group; and Muriel Agnes and Rose Johnson — all have been facilitators and friends.

A special thanks to Paige Prichard Kennedy for permission to use her art work, *Coding of a New Covenant in a Time of Crisis*. This book is merely commentary on her wondrous and profound mythic images.

My partner, Emily Kierstead, has taught me that music is an elemental force. The universe is music, vibration, energy — and singing is our soul's response to what the universe is telling us.. I thank her for the four of her songs included in this book. *Eve*, *Lament*, and *Holy of Holies* are on her CD, *Womanspirit* and she composed *It's Time* for the Millennium Celebration at Tatamagouche Centre. — and it has been popular ever since. The yang of the words need the yin of the music. Check the credit notes for how to contact either Paige or Emily.

Thanks also to all the people who helped with the preparation and production of this work. To Valerie Barrett, who helped bring my creative ventures in syntax and grammar into some kind of order. To Jim Taylor, whose editing from his depth of theological understanding and knowledge of the art and craft of writing greatly helped in creating a very readable finished work. (Valerie cleaned up the house making it presentable to the house cleaner, Jim!) To the Nova Scotia Self-Publishing Association, whose information and workshops introduced me to the possibilities and intricacies of self-publishing. To Richard Rogers of Glen Margaret Publishing who with good humour and professional skill did all the work of formatting and preparing this work for publication. To Brenda Conroy, whose sharp eye and graphic design skills created the cover.

Introduction

1

Exile
(2 Kings; Isaiah 35-55)

She's thirty-something, married with two children, intelligent, ambitious, with a yearning for a spiritual home that speaks to her soul. She goes to church on occasion, and sends her children, but finds there no nourishment that speaks to the depths within her.

He's in his late forties and approaching burnout. His years in the work world have been strenuous and demanding, and he's now searching for some deeper meaning and purpose in his life. He grew up in the church but does not consider returning there to find the spiritual solace he needs.

I, a minister of the United Church of Canada in my sixties, share with them — and the stories could go on and on — the feeling of exile. As citizens of the world, we find ourselves exiled from a church that has not kept pace.

Exile is a chilling word. It conjures up images of being removed from your home, your country, all the things that give life meaning. We think of refugees banished from their homelands and catch a glimpse of how devastating, bewildering, and discouraging that must be.

We do not choose exile. It is forced upon us. No one consults us nor considers our wishes. We find ourselves cut off from the familiar with few guideposts. Spiritually, we are in exile.

I experienced exile in relation to theology. My inherited belief system, including a seminary education, became an uncomfortable place that did not feel like home. Yet at some level I knew that I belonged with the church, and must work with its thinking. However, in its traditional form I find much of it a foreign land, not a place in which I can find life.

11

Israel's exile

The Bible gives us a classic case of an exile that was both physical and spiritual. It was the most traumatic experience in the history of the Hebrew people. About 586 BCE, a final wave of deportation signalled the devastation and destruction of their country, centred on Jerusalem and the temple. Deportation was the policy of their conquerors. A country is much easier to control if you remove large numbers of its people, particularly the leadership. Thus, the core of Israel found themselves in exile in Babylon.

We find it hard to imagine how tragic that experience must have been. They had been a people with a purpose. They knew the stories of their ancestors. They believed the promise of God that "I will make of you a great nation." (Genesis 12:2) They had escaped slavery in Egypt, endured the wilderness, and come to the Promised Land. Year by year, through the ritual of the Passover, they celebrated their feat. They knew their God was powerful, more powerful than all other gods. What other people had gone from slavery to nationhood?

Now, suddenly, they were exiles, cut off from everything that mattered: their land, their city, their temple, and even Yahweh their God. They could not imagine that Yahweh would ever allow such a thing to happen, but it had happened. Yahweh had failed. Their God was dead. We can understand them saying, "By the rivers of Babylon — there we sat down and there we wept when we remembered Zion." (Psalm 137:1)

Similarities with our exile

Their experience of exile is a lens through which we can see our own spiritual situation. The world we thought we knew has changed. What happened to the booming church of the 1950s? What happened to a culture that took its cues from the church? What happened to a faith that provided answers rather than questions, peace rather than dilemmas? The church, for many, no longer provides our longed-for connection with depth. Our souls find no abiding home. We are exiled. Some of us lived through the exile (the upheaval of the 1960s and '70s); those a bit younger were simply born into it.

Christians of many types feel exiled from the church. Conservatives feel that things are changing so fast they can't keep up. For liberals, change happens too slowly. All feel that the church has abandoned them. The church as a whole has been exiled from society — an ever decreasing minority relegated to the fringes. God has long since ceased being a subject of public discussion.

People survive exile.

For the Israelites, along came the writer of the mid portion of Isaiah (Isaiah 40-55) saying, "Comfort, O comfort my people, says your God." (Isaiah 40:1) Weeping there by the rivers of Babylon, they needed a word of comfort. They had been told often enough that they were there because of their sins. Now they heard, "Speak tenderly to Jerusalem, and cry to her that she has served her term, that her penalty is paid, that she has received from the Lord's hand double for all her sins." (Isaiah 40:2)

They heard a new word. The guilt was cast away, the burden lifted. Now their ears were open to hear an enlarged vision of God. Yahweh was more than a local deity. "Have you not known? Have you not heard? The Lord is the everlasting God, the Creator of the ends of the earth . . . [Yahweh] gives power to the faint, and strengthens the powerless . . . Those who wait for the Lord shall renew their strength, they shall mount up with wings like eagles, they shall run and not be weary, they shall walk and not faint." (Isaiah 40:28-31)

Yahweh was transformed from a national deity to the universal God of all creation. Under the power of that vision the Israelites survived. With a broadened faith they returned to their homeland to carry on their life. Even then it was not a story of "living happily ever after," but they did survive the crisis.

A renewed vision

Will we survive our crisis?

In the same way, a renewed vision is growing among us. Many stirrings in church and society witness to an awakening awareness of the great Mystery. Many spiritual streams now nourish our lives. Native spirituality has found a place. World religions, ancient and modern, are being explored as never before. "New age" spirituality testifies to a genuine yearning. Our modern world has brought old ways of thinking to an end, but has also opened the door to a new profound and relevant probing of the Mystery.

As an exile, now awakened to an enlarged vision, I wish to add my word. The bane and blessing of my life has been the inner compulsion, or the call of God, to think about these things. I am an apologist for the Christian faith; one who uses the thinking of our time — as Christians have always done — to help make the powerful truth of the Christian tradition more real and relevant.

The time for rebuilding has come. Join the journey.

Reflection questions

1. What is your experience of exile?
2. What was born out of your exile experience?
3. Can you imagine what exile has been like for other people in other situations?

Your thoughts

2
What is the Bible about?
(Genesis 1-4)

The best place to start exploring the meaning of the Bible is where the Bible starts, with its two mythic accounts of creation.

The opening words of the first chapter of Genesis give the first clue that a BIG story beckons us: "In the beginning. . ." (Genesis 1:1) You can't get farther back than that. The next word is "God," who is clearly a major player. Any story involves action, and we are not disappointed. God does something; "God created." More specifically, "God created the heavens and the earth" — the universe.

The stage is set. The players are God and the universe, the creative energy and the creation. This is a cosmic story.

The question is, What will God do with this creation?

A good creation

Creation starts out as a "formless void." This is a good description of the universe a short time after the Big Bang — but let us not confuse a wondrous mythic tale with science. "And darkness covered the face of the deep" (Genesis 1:2) introduces an ominous note. Certainly the words "darkness" and "deep" convey a sense of mystery and danger.

When we encounter darkness, we want light, so God turned on the light. "God said, 'Let there be light'; and there was light." (Genesis 1:3)

God continues creating. The earth and the sky get sorted out. Sea and land are separated. Vegetation begins. Day and night introduce a daily rhythm. Fish, including "the great sea monsters," appear. Birds fill the sky, and animals the land. (Genesis 1:6-25)

God's final creation is very special — human beings. The same Hebrew word used for the original creation is used again here. "Let us make humankind in our image . . . and let them have dominion over" (a better translation might be "responsibility for") all the earth and its creatures. (Genesis 1:26)

Thus Genesis introduces humankind as another stage of creation having the potential and responsibility of being partners with God within the rest of creation. (Genesis 1:26-30)

Having completed creation, "God saw everything that [God] had made, and indeed, it was very good." (Genesis 1:31)

Problems emerge

Life, however, is not that simple. The second creation myth, actually written before the first one, introduces the problem. The second account of creation begins a few verses into the second chapter of Genesis.

Adam is created and placed in an idyllic garden "to till it and keep it." (Genesis 2:15b) Eve is later created from a rib of Adam to be "his partner." (Genesis 2:18b) They are total innocents, living in a luxurious garden which provides all their needs. In that state, they are incapable of taking responsibility for themselves, let alone the earth. Like children, they need to grow up, become mature, and learn who they are and what their responsibility is.

The story makes clear that creation is a work in progress.

The Bible, and history, is the story of our slow, faltering, often disastrous attempts to grow up, to become what we were created to be. We are not there yet. A new millennium has dawned, but the problem of our immaturity, introduced in the opening chapters of the Bible, remains. In fact it has grown and now threatens our survival. Will we grow up sufficiently before we completely destroy ourselves and our world?

The Bible presents mature humanity as a possibility and a mythic hope. In the opening myths of creation and awakening, Genesis spells out the "human condition," our continued existence challenged by our own darkness. In the closing myths of Revelation, we have the vision of our fulfilment, a new heaven and a new earth. In between is the long, slow, painful struggle of a particular people as they (we) strive to become whole.

The Bible as the personal journey

We can read the Bible as our personal journey, for we are all in the process of growing up.

We all start out as Eve. We all bite the fruit – that is, we wake up to the possibilities of life. We all go through an Exodus experience — we leave home, go through wildernesses, and arrive at promised lands. As Israel became a kingdom, so we set out to make our mark — have a career, raise a family. Many have a mid-life crisis, like the Exile of Israel. Some come to the wisdom of the mature years — the Jesus story. A few attain to the final marriage of flesh and spirit, symbolized as the New Jerusalem of the book of Revelation.

Life, however, does not usually move neatly from stage to stage. We have many an exodus and exile, but often we find in the biblical accounts that which reflects the various phases and movements within our lives.

The Bible as the human journey

We must also read the Bible as the human story.

The Bible is the story of a people, not just of individuals. The New Jerusalem is a community, not an individual. The fulfilment of Revelation's vision of a new heaven and a new earth is a communal effort. It can come about only when "all of us come . . . to maturity, to the measure of the full stature of Christ." (Ephesians 4:13) Individualistic interpretations of Christianity are not adequate.

We can read all history in the light of the Bible. The world has many wildernesses, kingdoms and exiles, as well as many Christ figures. Oppression and injustice are the lot of most of humanity. Wars and threats of war are a constant.

Yet all history is the raw material for our growth and a challenge to take what responsibility we can. As we take more and more responsibility for the havoc wrought by our collective immaturity and the possibilities of what humanity can become, we become more fully what we were created to be. Individually and collectively, we grow in the crucible of history.

The Bible as God's journey

God cannot be left out of this picture. The Hebrews were keenly aware of their relationship with the Source. They felt surrounded by a divine presence which called them, and which judged them when they failed to respond. We meet a passionate God who yearns for a mature and responsible people, but who sometimes acts immaturely and irresponsibly when they fall short!

It seems that God can grow to the fullness of being God only through having a suitable partner, a free and responsible creature made in God's image. God grows as we grow. We mature as God matures. The traditional image of a changeless God has become one of a growing God. This is Carl Jung's insight, explored most fully in his book *Answer to Job*. It is a new thought for many – exciting for some, disturbing for others. The church has started to take note. For example, one of Brian Wren's new hymns (268 in *Voices United*, the new hymn book of the United Church of Canada) gives us "Young, growing God, eager, on the move."

So the Bible is also about God becoming fully God — a mythic and cosmic journey.

If this is true, and I believe it is, then our ultimate purpose and challenge is to partner God in bringing full consciousness to creation. We can do so only by becoming fully mature, free and responsible creatures.

The Bible is the story of our moving toward that end, as individuals, as humanity, and as the growing heart of God.

Reflection questions

1. What do you hope to gain from reading this book?
2. What thoughts resonate with your own thinking?
3. Are there any thoughts that are troublesome or offensive?

Your thoughts

Note

1. Quoting, in slightly different context, the title of Marcus Borg's book, *Meeting Jesus Again For the First Time*.

Eve

Eve

Let me tell you about Eve,
Eve was not what you believe,
Eve was quite a gal!
Let me tell you about Eve,
For I think you've been deceived.
Eve was quite a gal!
Eve was burnin', Eve was burnin'
to be more than Adam's wife.

Let me tell you about Eve,
Eve was not what you believe.
Eve was quite a gal!
Let me tell you about Eve,
For I think you've been deceived
Eve was quite a gal!
Eve was yearnin' Eve was yearnin'
Eve was yearnin' for her life!

Now Eve was good, and Eve was smart,
Although she'd never been to college.
You must agree, she did her part
to share with us the fruit of knowledge!
Poor Eve, poor Eve,
Good Eve, smart Eve,
Let me tell you about Eve...

Now Eve was good, and Eve was smart,
before she covered up her bareness..
You must agree, she did her part
to bring us humans to awareness!
Poor Eve, poor Eve,
Good Eve, smart Eve.
Let me tell you about Eve...

The Mystery, the Holy One,
had given Eve a tantalizer.
She ate, and innocence was gone
The outcome surely did surprise her!
Poor Eve, poor Eve,
Good Eve, smart Eve,
                    Emily Kierstead

3
Celebrating Eve
(Genesis 3-4)

The time has come to unabashedly celebrate Eve.

We must do more than stop blaming her for all the ills of humanity. This curse that has shadowed womanhood throughout the Judeo-Christian tradition must end. And we can do it.

We are now at a place where we can see the Garden of Eden myth with fresh eyes. With the mortal wounding of patriarchy — but remember how dangerous wounded creatures can be — we can look more deeply into this wondrous story of our beginnings, and in the process transform Eve from villain to heroine.

At least as far back as my days in Seminary, we were talking about the "fall upward," but we stopped far short of celebrating Eve as the mythic heroine who made it possible. Understanding this story as the awakening of consciousness — and reading the whole Bible as the story of our growing maturity — required a deeper rethinking than I, or anyone I knew about, could manage at that time.

The untruthful God

But times have changed. We can now understand that the God represented in this story is not an ultimate model of divinity. We can question God's command, "You may freely eat of every tree of the garden; but of the tree of the knowledge of good and evil you shall not eat, for in the day that you eat of it you shall die." (Genesis 2:16-17)

Calling God a liar may sound a little strong, but certainly the God pictured here misrepresents the truth. We must ask, "Is there something wrong with 'knowing good and evil', with growing up and becoming mature?" Surely it is the essence of our nature to want to know and understand, to grow and become.

Eve symbolizes the first glimmering awareness that life involves more than lying around in a garden enjoying the luscious fruit that falls into her lap. Eve is each of us as a young child who basks in the warmth, love and good will of her family. Yet like every child, she is curious and wants to know and grow.

However, the God we meet in this creation story in Genesis will have none of it. This God is fearful, even jealous, of the creature fashioned as a reflection of God's own divinity. God seems shocked that mortals have "become like one of us, knowing good and evil," so much so that they must be evicted from the Garden lest they "take also from the tree of life, and eat, and live forever." (Genesis 3:22)

In other words, Eve incurred the anger of God by being true to who she was created to be! This God must be seen not as the ultimate divinity but as the creation of a patriarchy dismayed by human folly and fearful of the power of women.

The truthful serpent

Another little twist to the Garden story is that, in this interpretation, the snake becomes the bearer of truth. The serpent is a better god-image than God!

"Now the serpent was more crafty than any other wild animal that the Lord God had made." After a conversation with Eve regarding the forbidden fruit, the serpent assured her, "You will not die; for God knows when you eat of it your eyes will be opened, and you will be like God, knowing good and evil." (Genesis 3:1, 4-5) Which is, in fact, exactly what happened. By contrast, God said they would die, and they didn't — or at least, not immediately.

In most traditions, the serpent is a positive symbol of life and transformation. Here, however, the serpent is pictured as the crafty tempter of Eve. When we realize that this myth emerged from a paranoid patriarchal tradition, we need not be surprised that the snake (a feminine image) appears as a tempter. Taking away the patriarchal overlay, we can reinstate the serpent as the knowing sharer of truth who encourages Eve to enter into the possibilities of life.

"So when the woman saw that the tree was good for food, and that it was a delight to the eyes, and that the tree was to be desired to make one wise, she took of its fruit and ate; and she also gave some to her husband, who was with her, and he ate." (Genesis 3:6) When confronted with this desirable, erotic, delightful fruit — the enticement of life — she ate it, as any normal person would.

Eve took the giant step which set humanity on the road to becoming full, conscious, aware, mature partners of God; a journey which, according to the Christian myth, will not end until the arrival of the perfect fulfilment of a new heaven and a new earth.

Sin is still real

Unfortunately, this is a long and hard journey. History, with all its glory and woe, is the story of its unfolding. As individuals, our road to maturity is often difficult and never complete. We must contend with the reality of evil as the dark side of growing up.

Not surprisingly, we have read the story of the Garden as "The Fall" because it spells out in excruciating and painful detail the grim results of opening the door to growth. Adam and Eve become separated, within themselves and from one another: "Then the eyes of both were opened, and they knew that they were naked." (Genesis 3:7) And from the earth: "By the sweat of your face you shall eat bread." (Genesis 3:19) And finally, from God: "The man and his wife hid themselves from the presence of the Lord God." (Genesis 3:8b)

This state of separation we call sin, and sin has dire consequences. The very next story leads to Cain slaying Abel, brother slaying brother — the human reality ever since. The Bible, including the Garden myth, is correct in taking sin very, very seriously. Sin is the abiding evidence that we are on the journey but have not yet arrived.

The painful but wonderful journey

The Christian myth, from creation and awakening to the final reuniting in the New Jerusalem, presents the tough and amazing drama of moving from the innocent unity of the Garden to knowing oneness within the New Jerusalem.

So let us celebrate Eve, the heroine who set us on our journey. Difficulty and pain haunt the trip. But it is life; exhilarating and fulfilling in a way that the sweet innocence of the Garden can never match.

Reflection questions

1. Are there aspects of the above interpretation of the Garden of Eden myth that excite and/or trouble you?
2. Recall some moments from your childhood when a light went on for you.
3. What are some good, and perhaps not so good, things that resulted from these experiences?

Your thoughts

4
It's only a myth?
(Luke 11:24-26)

What myth are you living?

Not so many years ago, I would have found that question silly, if not offensive. I had never thought of my life as living out, or within, a myth. We used to assume that a myth is a story that is not true. How many times have you said, "It's only a myth," meaning that it (whatever "it" is) is not real? I do it all the time, even though I'm beginning to know better.

Our changing understanding of myth

Our understanding of myth has completely turned around since my young days. We didn't focus much on myth in those days. I suppose we had some of the stories of Greek mythology in our literature courses, but we gave no thought to the truth value they might contain. Any myths we read were part of ancient religions which were, we assumed, false. Christianity had replaced all that mythology stuff with a real religion that told of things that had actually happened!

In Seminary, we did become aware that we could rarely rely on the historic accuracy of the biblical accounts. We even discovered that myth occasionally got mixed up in it. We also learned that myth should be weeded out. The historic setting and all the usual apparatus of biblical interpretation occupied us, but myth was not part of it. Rudolf Bultmann's *Kerygma and Myth* made it really clear that we have to cut away the dross of myth in order to get at the real teachings of Jesus.

Then came Joseph Campbell who, along with others, introduced western culture to the universal reality of myth. Every religion, culture, tribe, country, tradition has evolved a mythology. And these mythologies have many similarities. *The Hero With A Thousand Faces* tells us that every tradition has a path to wholeness and destiny. *The Masks of God* introduces the many ways God is represented and understood.

A whole new world opens up. The stories of mythology are not only interesting tales of the cavorting of gods and goddesses; they were a means of telling a people who they were and what their lives were about. We can imagine the tribe sitting around the campfire listening to the storyteller and feeling that they were within the drama. They met gods and heroes with whom they could identify. Their lives were about living out the myth.

Our myths

We, of course, feel very superior to these ancient mythologies. In our modern, rational world, where we turn to science and technology for our solutions, what need have we of myth?

Yet we sit in front of the television and watch the sitcoms, which have their appeal because they are all various tellings of the American, or western cultural, myth. We read novels. We get caught up in movies. We worship our superstars as the ancients did their gods — why else would we pay millions to our sports heroes for bashing one another around? Look at the mythology around Elvis. "Star Wars" is simply a modern version of the ancient and universal mythic theme of good versus evil. Myth surrounds us.

Even with all this evidence, only reluctantly do we own up to the power of myth in our lives. It goes against our scientific mindset. We would be embarrassed to admit that our mythologies are anything more than entertainment. Culture, however, moves on, and we are getting over our unwillingness to connect life and myth. We slowly begin to grasp the reality that myths still shape our lives.

Choosing our myths

The question now is not whether myths shape our lives, but which myths? Some myths lead to life, and some do not. Our lives and our psyches are the battleground for contending myths. We have come to understand that the intrigues, affairs, and battles of the mythic realm are the projections of our inner world. In myths, our competing instincts, demands, dreams, responsibilities, and expectations all call out for attention. Sorting them out is not easy.

We ignore myths at our peril, and our culture is indeed in peril because we have ignored our myths. We have lost our conscious connection with the deep archetypal myths that have given meaning and purpose to human life. Without any grand myth to lift us beyond ourselves, we tend to get caught up in the shallow myths of pleasure, sex, money, things, food, nationalism, power, etc. These can be frighteningly demonic. In the hands of Hitler the myth of the superior race had dire consequences.

Without a depth connection, any of the above myths can become ends in themselves rather than aspects of life. For example, when we, or our pension funds, invest money, we tend to get caught up in the money market myth that only making money matters. Most of us give little thought to how our money serves the human good. We forget another mythology that says if we "strive first for the kingdom [the deep purpose of our lives] . . . all these things will be given to you as well." (Matthew 6:33)

We become so easily submerged in our culture that we fail to notice the myths that live within us and form our unconscious assumptions about life and its purpose. The parable of the unclean spirit (Luke 11:24-26) makes clear that when the old spirits (myths) go, there is a vacuum. We become vulnerable to whatever comes along, and the new ones may be "more evil . . . and the last state of that person is worse than the first."

A time of hope

Ours, though, is a time of hope.

We are beginning to recognize that the surface myths we have adopted fail to satisfy our deep spiritual needs. I believe the present yearning and searching for "spirituality" represents our hunger for methods and myths that connect us to the deep sources and realities of life. It is a great sign of hope.

I believe that Christianity, which our culture has swept out, can return as a living myth for our time. The goal of this book is to help it happen.

We need to listen to the stories and enter the myths that give depth and meaning to our lives.

Reflection questions

1. What is the truth within the Santa Claus myth?
2. What are some false myths which influence you?
3. Are there books, stories, characters, events that you find powerful and affirming?

Your thoughts

5
The Christian myth
(Genesis, Revelation)

Do the words "Christian" and "mythology" belong together? I still feel a certain inner twinge when I say "Christian mythology," as if I am doing something wrong — an unfortunate carry-over from my past!

Certainly my theological education did not encourage thinking of Christianity as mythology. I agreed at that time with the generally accepted view that other religions were based on mythology, but not Christianity. Christianity, we believed, was founded on historic fact and therefore has grown beyond mythology.

The Bible as mythology

Gradually it dawned on me that the Bible not only contains mythology, it *is* a mythology. True, it presents us with the history and literature of a particular tradition, but the events described create a Big Story, a grand and complete mythology. In my student days, I would have thought that such a statement was the ultimate blasphemy. How things have changed!

The Bible begins and ends in pure mythology. No one was around to document creation. So in no way can the Genesis stories be a literal account of what happened. In the same way, the Revelation visions are not literal descriptions of actual events that ever did or ever will happen.

The stories of creation and fulfilment that begin and end the Bible are clear examples of myth as meaning-giving stories. In the first account of creation we have a dramatic and compelling telling of an evolving universe. It culminates in the creation of humanity: the creature made responsible for the earth. It affirms that "God saw everything that [God] had made, and indeed, it was very good." (Genesis 1:31)

Humanity, however, is an unfinished work. To be truly creatures in the "image of God," they must become as "gods"; they must grow to be fully aware, moral, responsible, creative, loving, creatures able to partner God in our time and space universe. The Bible gives us one tradition's story of that journey to wholeness.

The Garden of Eden story sets the stage. Eve exercises her free will by acting against the expressed wish of God and eating the forbidden fruit. This first move toward becoming the "image of God," the step into consciousness, initiates all the turmoil of human history. In the Christian mythology, and (we hope) in our experience, history is the arena where we can grow into godlikeness.

The vision of a better world and more glorious future gives us hope and draws us on. In the Bible this yearning appears as a series of mythic visions which lure the people forward: the promised land, a new king David, a Messiah, a Kingdom of God, a new heaven and new earth. With each new experience they learn something new. They grow. Their ideas about life and God expand and change until the fullness of God and humanity appear in the end as the new heaven and new earth.

The visions of Revelation picture the grim route toward, and the final achieving of, the new humanity. Evil is overcome, the separations and divisions caused by the awakening of consciousness are healed, and the marriage of heaven and earth takes place. In the final images, the New Jerusalem descends "coming down out of heaven from God." (Revelation 21:2b) The healing waters flow freely: "Let everyone who wishes take the water of life as a gift." (22:17b) And the faithful "have the right to the tree of life." (22:14)

These great myths of consummation pull us toward our ultimate destiny where the New Jerusalem represents humanity fulfilled.

History and myth

We think of history and myth as very separate and distinct things. Actually, they are interwoven. Each creates the other. Mythology emerges from experience (history) and, since we always want to translate our myths into real life, history shapes future experience. History, then, gives us the story of the evolving and living out of a mythology that urges humanity toward what we are capable of being.

In this sense, the Christian mythology is the same as all other mythologies. They have emerged from history and then seek to become real in history. *The Iliad* and *The Odyssey,* for example, emerge from the dim beginnings of Greek history as the founding mythology of Greek civilization. The great stories about battles and beautiful women (Helen of Troy), about heroes and villains, gave meaning and purpose to the Greek world.

As one of the major influences on western civilization, these myths also help to shape us and our culture. The adventures and tribulations of Odysseus on his way home to Ithaca become the journey we all make as we come home to our true selves.

Inheritors Of The Christian Myth

No doubt humanity needs the truth that comes from all mythologies. My part of the task, however, is to explore the truth within the Christian myth. I want to have some small part in retelling the Christian myth in modern dress. Since Christianity, along with Greek civilization, has provided the undergirding myth of western culture, we are all its inheritors, whether we claim any connection with Christianity or not. We need to be familiar with it and use it as we can.

Our modern world has largely forgotten the depth and power of myth and has succumbed to a shallow mythology of pleasure and greed. Babylon beckons. That path, however, leads to destruction.

The real issue is whether we can enter the New Jerusalem and reach a higher level of maturity, awareness, and consciousness before we extinguish human life upon this planet. By awakening to mythic power, including the Christian myth, we can again allow the depths of our lives to be drawn into the drama of human becoming.

Reflection questions

1. What are some dreams that you would like to make into reality?
2. What is the difference between the Bible *containing* myth and *being* a myth?
3. State the biblical myth in your own words.

Your thoughts

6
What? A three-level universe?
(A conceptual framework for understanding the Bible and life)

I've come full circle.

As a child, like most others from a religious home, I inherited the old image of a three- level universe with heaven up there, the earth here, and hell — or some such place — under the earth. In my adult years, that model ceased to make sense for me and left me floundering. Now, in my later years, I'm back to believing in three orders of reality that mould our lives. It's been a long journey.

Physics always wins

They say physics always wins.

The idea of a three-level universe had died long before I came on the scene. Copernicus did it in, centuries ago, but the echoes of his discovery linger on. He figured out that the earth goes around the sun. This meant that, in physical reality, there was an "up there" but no "down there" — no place for hell. So we ceased to take hell, the devil, and even evil, seriously.

When the sun became a minor star in a vast universe, the notion of "up there" also became vague. We had come to accept the basic outlook of Newtonian physics, which says that the universe operates mechanically like a giant clock. Perhaps it needs something from another dimension to get it started, but once in motion, the universe can run on its own. In that system, there is no need for God. Thus, in western culture, the idea of God has also grown dimmer and dimmer.

I'm actually describing what happened to me in my early adult years.

The battle within me raged between my childhood three-level universe, which ceased to make any sense for me, and a Newtonian universe that had no need of God. Newton had to win. That left me locked into a mechanical universe in which science could solve all problems and God was a vague something relegated to the fringes of life. Finally, in my early thirties, I had to admit that the God I had inherited had, for me, died — a tough place to live when you have to preach every Sunday!

While in this dark period, I discovered Transactional Analysis, which kept me alive in the wilderness. The realization that TA could be a vehicle for the exploration of faith presented me with a whole new vista for exploration. This eventually resulted in my first book, *For Unbelieving Christians.* I now think I should have called it *Survival In The Wilderness*, for TA proved effective for telling the Christian story on the human level but it provided no conceptual framework for speaking of the divine or other realms of reality.

Spirit/Matter

Fortunately, the world keeps moving on.

We now know that science has not solved our basic problems (e.g., How can we learn to love one another?) and we have lost faith that it ever will. At the same time, science itself has moved on and left Newtonian physics far behind. (But you had better continue to believe Newton, especially if you drive a car; those laws really do work!)

The particle physicists now sound like mystics. We hear that matter is not the basic stuff of the universe; energy is. Energy is not random or neutral; it seems to have will or purpose of its own. Energy wants to unite with other energy/matter. The religious term for this is spirit. Now the stuff of the universe is, as Teilhard de Chardin told us, spirit/matter.

Our minds boggle. Giving up the security of a Newtonian universe where matter is matter, and spirit is something dragged in by the theologians, can be very shattering.

But physics gives us only part of the story.

Over the years, I discovered mythology (Joseph Campbell) and depth psychology (Carl Jung). I enjoyed exploring some physicists who write for the lay person.. I searched as diligently as I could for something that could begin to make sense out of the swirl of the rise of the feminine, the spiritual, mythology, depth psychology, the new physics and whatever else was going. Nor did I ever abandon the Bible and theology as a source of meaning.

Then came another great flash of light.

It happened while reading Jean Houston's[1] book, *The Search For The Beloved*. As she sorted out levels of reality, I suddenly knew that she had unearthed a conceptual framework, a way of thinking, that made sense for me, and, I believe, for our time. Everything I know about can fit into it. Attending her Mystery School[2] was a jump-start toward integrating this new thinking into my being and my thinking.

Back to a three-level universe

Out of her research (under the auspices of the American government) into the effects of LSD, her exploration of the ancient and modern sacred traditions of the earth, and her experience with many people, Jean Houston discovered that our dreams, visions, and hallucinations sorted out into four categories: the sensate, the historic/psychological, the mythic/archetypal, and the Unitive.

This scheme can be pictured as concentric circles. The sensate and the historic/psychological – the here and now real-life experiences — form the inner circle.

The outer circle represents the Unitive level or order of reality. This is the home of God, Ultimate reality, the Source, the Oneness, or however we want to name that which is beyond naming. This supreme Mystery from which all emerges surrounds and permeates the universe, all life, everything.

Between the historic and the Unitive lies the mythic/archetypal realm. Here reside the gods and goddesses, heroes and heroines, spirits and demons, and all the creatures that people the mythic tales of the earth. In Jungian terms, this circle is the collective unconscious or the objective psyche, the home of the archetypes. In the Christian tradition, it is heaven.

Understanding this level, and accepting its reality and power, stretches our traditional thinking. It has taken centuries to move from the heaven-earth-hell mindset to accepting the Newtonian view as the natural order of things. I have no doubt that it will take generations to feel at home in this new vision of reality. We must, however, explore it as the great reservoir of all those larger-than-life energies of good and evil that constantly work on us and in us.

In this scheme, heaven and God are not far distant. Indeed, they surround and envelop us. They form the ocean we live in, the energies which shape and mould every moment of every life.

Reflection questions

1. Describe some moments, situations or places that brought great peace.
2. What is real for you?
3. Have you had experiences that could be called "mythic" or "mystic"?

Your thoughts

7
Heaven
(The mythic realm)

This three-realm universe I have introduced needs more exploration. Heaven, the mythic realm, the middle one in Jean Houston's scheme, seems the hardest for us to grasp. It differs too much from our traditional picture.

The disappearance of heaven

The message of my childhood pictured heaven as the home of God and the place we go, or don't go, when we die. We had to be good so we would go to heaven. Being good meant following the rules and regulations of parents, church, teachers, country, and whatever else represented authority. If no one else was around, God was keeping an eye on you, so escape was impossible. Santa Claus had much the same role as Christmas approached, but we never really doubted that Santa would come.

Over the years, heaven has receded into the background. We seldom hear sermons on it in our mainline churches. It is not constantly held before us as the chief goal and destiny of life. For many, it has lost all reality or has become a vague and distant place with little or no importance for everyday living.

For me, this leaves a vacuum. In spite of the downplaying of heaven there remains in me a fundamental, bedrock belief, deeper than reason or experience, that nothing is ultimately lost. I cannot imagine that a person's life simply disappears. There has to be some abiding reality to the lives of all who have gone before us. The quote from Hebrews about being "surrounded by so great a cloud of witnesses" (Hebrews 12:1), has always struck a deep chord within me.

Unfortunately, we have lost a language, a way of thinking, that could make such a place real for us.

The reappearance of heaven

As one way of thinking dies, another is being born.

Along came depth psychology, especially Carl Jung with his talk of archetypes, the collective unconscious, and such things. He introduced us to a whole inner world, another realm, that is as surely and powerfully real as our physical world of time and space. With that insight, heaven is transformed from a fading reality to an intimate and ever-present place that profoundly affects every thought and move of our lives.

Jung called this realm the collective unconscious or the objective psyche. He believed that each of us has a personal unconscious, a large part of ourselves which remains unknown to us. We are not, however, isolated and alone. At depth, we all connect to a large reservoir of all that humanity has been and can be. The universal patterns, images, and symbols that appear in religions, mythologies, and dreams witness to a common source.

Jung called particular patterns or energies "archetypes." Jung would say that we derive the enormous energy and focus required for twenty years of parenting from the parenting archetype. Mary the mother of Jesus is a mother image generated by the mother archetype — as is Demeter, the mother of Persephone, in Greek mythology. Princess Diana carried a princess archetype. King David embodied a ruler archetype.

These archetypal energies create the gods and goddesses, heroes and villains, of mythology. The complexity of their personalities and relationships give us a glimpse into the multitude of forces that contend within us and among us.

Is this heaven real?

Am I talking about something substantial, or do we merely imagine it? We can probably all accept mythology as the projections of a people's inner struggles and understandings. We can understand the gods and goddesses as energies that operate within and among us. But we still ask if there is anything objectively real in all this? Or does it exist only in our minds? If it exists in our minds, does that mean it is not real?

A tough question. For now, chew on the maxim that the pen is mightier than the sword. An idea has more power to influence us than any physical force.

The Christian belief in one God presents another stumbling block to this view of heaven. We have traditionally thought of heaven as the home of God. How does one God fit in with a place that teems with a multitude of gods?

Yes, heaven contains all sorts of spirits (archetypes), but a special one stands out, a Holy Spirit, a God archetype, that seeks to bring order, system and wholeness to the multitude of forces at work. Just as in our lives an energy pulls us toward wholeness, so also in the universe such an energy seems to operate. The Old Testament could see God presiding over a heavenly council, which expresses much the same scheme. This is not pure monotheism, but it pictures one God who calls the shots.

This heaven is not new

This concept of heaven has a long history. Jung merely modernized an idea that goes back at least as far as Plato. Plato spoke of an eternal realm of forms where we find the ideas or models from which all earthly things are created. Teilhard de Chardin wrote of the noosphere, an energy reservoir that encircles the earth and contains the energies of every human being that ever lived. In the realm of physics, Rupert Sheldrake talks about morphogenetic fields (form-creating energies), which seem a lot like archetypes. Then, too, the writer to the Hebrews tells us that "we are surrounded by so great a cloud of witnesses" (Hebrews 12:1) — the multitude of those who have died before us.

Much more could be said, but this is a start we can build on. I am, of course, dipping into a mystery, and I delude myself if I think I can personally fathom its depths. I feel impelled, however, to explore it as I can. How exhilarating to enter the venture!

Reflection questions

1. How important has heaven been for you?
2. Who are your favourite characters, gods, goddesses, in myths and stories known to you?
3. Does it excite or trouble you to think of Christianity as another mythology among the mythologies of the earth?

Your thoughts

8
Heaven is real
(General background)

Understanding heaven as a presence in our lives may still be a major challenge for you. Let me delve into it a bit more.

Heaven has been so central to Christian belief that having to talk about its nature and reality seems strange. We have seen, however, and know from our own experience, that the idea of heaven has been largely lost to our modern world.

I want to make clear that heaven is close, "nearer than hands and feet, closer than breathing" (a traditional prayer). As I have said, every level of our three-reality universe surrounds us every moment of every day. The mystic level, the thirst for life, Eros, constantly meets us as Mystery and yearning. We bump into our flesh-and-blood world at every turn — and we truly accept its reality. Heaven, the mythic realm, the home of gods and goddesses, heroes and villains, has the most impact in giving particular shape to our lives. It is, however, the one most difficult for us to accept as real.

Where do ideas live?

The realm of thinking and ideas can give us a "rational" way to approach the reality of heaven.

I commented earlier that the pen is mightier than the sword. Words, thoughts, ideas, concepts, can carry mythic power. People have gone to war and slaughtered one another with great abandon for the sake of an idea. The cry, "Give me liberty or give me death," impelled many to go to their deaths. Never underestimate the power of an idea.

Where do such thoughts come from? Where do they reside?

It's not enough to say that a thought resides only in my head. The same thought can reside in many heads. A thought, a fad, an ideology, or a mythology, can take over whole groups or nations of people. Look what the idea of "the superior race" did in the hands of Hitler. Such ideas take on a life of their own, a much larger life than the thought of any individual, or even of all the individuals who hold it.

The hundredth monkey

Have you heard of the hundredth monkey experiment? In my memory, it goes like this. A group of monkeys, living on an island, is fed by bananas thrown along the sand. Even monkeys don't enjoy eating sand-covered bananas. One day a monkey gets a great idea and washes her banana in the sea before eating it. After a while, another monkey copies the first one. Slowly, the number who wash their bananas grows. At a certain point, all the rest catch on. Even monkeys on neighbouring islands, who have no direct connection with the first group, spontaneously start washing their bananas.

We can easily understand the process by which an idea, a concept, suddenly catches on. What had been strange and new suddenly becomes accepted wisdom. We have seen it happen among humans many times. More baffling is the fact that other monkeys on other islands, who had no connection with the first group, started doing the same thing. How did the idea get from one group to the other?

Other experiments have demonstrated the same phenomenon. Once mice learn their way through a maze in one part of the world, mice in the rest of the world can learn the same maze much more quickly. Similar discoveries are made in different places without collaboration! How come?

There seems to be a pool of thought or ideas to which we are all connected.

Morphogenetic fields

Rupert Sheldrake, the biochemist whom I have mentioned, talks of such energy existing as morphogenetic fields. You can read about it in his books, such as *The Presence of the Past*. Morphogenetic means "form-creating". A morphogenetic field is an energy that works toward some form or end. There is, for example, an energy of leadership. We know something of how leaders operate because of all those who exercised leadership before us. Some magnet seems to attract the energies having to do with leadership. Every time leadership happens, this energy grows. This in turn influences all subsequent leadership. We feed the morphogenetic fields, and they feed us.

Every person, family, culture, religion, nation, or group of any kind develops a particular set of morphogenetic fields. They are a reality within which we live. Such fields surround us. They act as the forming forces of our lives.

The idea of morphogenetic fields sounds much the same as Jung's concept of the collective unconscious and archetypes.

An archetype, like a morphogenetic field, is the container, magnet, or creative engine that attracts a type of energy. Continuing the example of leadership, the energy of leadership builds up through the lived experience of that particular aspect of life. Every culture will have its own leadership archetypes. They will be different in detail from those of other cultures, but there will always be a leadership archetype (or morphogenetic field) which shapes leadership.

Heaven surrounds us

When Christians talk about heaven, when mythologists talk about the mythic realm, when depth psychology talks about the collective unconscious, and scientists — a few anyway — talk about morphogenetic fields, I claim that they all refer to the same reality. They represent various ways of looking at the same thing.

I believe that these ways of thinking have rescued heaven from oblivion. Depth psychology has connected the mythic realm to our psychic inner world of dreams, fantasies, etc. Heaven resides within us as well as beyond us.

Physics and the study of form-creating energy fields give the mythic/heavenly realm even more credibility. Suddenly, a vague and misty realm is brought close. What had the most tenuous connection with our everyday life is now the ocean in which we swim.

The re-emergence of the mythic/heavenly realm means two things. First, a realm that contains the energies, thoughts, myths, symbols and dreams of life really exists. Second, this realm intimately intermeshes with our daily lives. In it "we live and move and have our being." (Acts 17:28)

By implication, everything we are and do matters eternally. Our being and actions enter this mythic realm and join the energies of all who have gone before us. Our lives add, or fail to add, our particular shape and energy to the archetypes that will then help to shape the lives of all who come after. We receive the gift of the past, and our lives become a gift to all future generations.

In this age, when we either carry on to our own destruction or come to another level of consciousness, we want our gift to be full and complete.

Reflection questions

1. What ideas, visions, causes, have motivated you?
2. What are some evil forces that threaten our world?
3. It what ways do you build up the good energies?

Your thoughts

9
The creation of Yahweh
(The God of the Bible)

Here comes a big one. It's time to examine the creation of Yahweh
— a foreign thought in our traditional belief system.

Yahweh as archetype

I have already hinted that the God we meet in the Bible both *is*
and *is not* the Ultimate God. Yahweh, the primary name given to
the God of the Bible, and the Ultimate God represent different
orders of reality. Yahweh lives in heaven, the mythic/archetypal
level, while Ultimate Mystery, the primary force, intent, or purpose of the universe, forms the third or Unitive level. In Jungian
terms, Yahweh would be the god-image of the Hebrew people. As
such, Yahweh *represents* the Ultimate but is not the Ultimate. In
Joseph Campbell's phrase, Yahweh is a mask of God, one of many
masks or mythic representations of the Ultimate.

How are god-images, or the mythologies that contain them,
created?

Developing god-images is the natural response to the universal awareness of a presence, a force, an other, that is both within
us and over against us. Every culture does it. Only in our modern,
science-based, secular world have we come close to losing our
mystic awareness. Being human means being aware that we live
within Mystery.

We give shape and reality to the Mystery by evolving mythologies. We do it by projecting the forces and energies that work
in us and among us onto the mythic realm. Our wonderfully interesting and complex mythologies reflect who we are.

Every tradition and culture produces its own mythology. Particular historic experience gives a special flavour to each one. Much
of life, however, is the same for all humanity, so mythologies have
many similarities. Each one is unique, and yet has much in common with others in how it gives expression to the Mystery.

The Hebrews were like every other culture in their need to evolve a god-image. The Ultimate worked in them as in everyone and everything else. Yahweh, the name Moses heard at the burning bush, appeared as a god-image out of the tension, dialogue, or communion between the Ultimate level and the Hebrew people.

Hebrew uniqueness: monotheism

Hebrew uniqueness lies in the kind of god-image that developed; a monotheism rather than a polytheism. (They are not alone in being monotheists, but, interestingly enough, the three major monotheistic religions — Jewish, Muslim and Christian — share a common early history).

Monotheism means there is one God, or one God above all others. "You shall have no other gods before me" (Exodus 20:3) was the command to the Hebrew people. This is another way of saying one issue or theme dominates life. One particular force or energy becomes the focus above all others.

This single-mindedness is both the power and problem of monotheism. If one force dominates, what about all the others?

Polytheism solves the problem by having all sorts of gods and goddesses, heroes and villains, who represent a multitude of forces or archetypes. This honours the complexity and diversity of our lives, but the problem of singling out a central or most important aspect of life remains.

Monotheism chooses the opposite tack by saying there is one central issue to which we must attend.

What is this one dominant energy or issue? Once again we must probe our own nature, and the same answer comes back. Our thirst for life, our yearning, is what motivates us. Our Eros nature not only wants to live, but to live well and fully.

Polytheists will define living fully as having a great variety of life experiences, but not necessarily with a particular focus or direction. Monotheists define living fully as being our true selves in the world. The strength of polytheism is that the multitude of life's possibilities are spread before us. The power of monotheism is that the focus is on becoming whole, on growth, on offering to the world our uniqueness.

With polytheism, pleasure or entertainment can easily become our goal. Or we can get lost among all the contending possibilities and necessities of life, rather than growing or being transformed. In monotheism, the dialogue is between God and us, between the self we can be and the person we are. This means that we are constantly pressured toward growth. We may, however, become narrow and dull by losing sight of the breadth and possibilities of life.[3]

Monotheism, however, has another dangerous downside: the ease with which we can identify our particular version of truth with "The Truth." All religions are prone to fundamentalism — my truth is the only truth — but it is especially virulent among monotheisms. The fundamentalist side of the three monotheisms present a great danger to our world, especially when it gains political power.

Yahweh's evolution

At one level, the Bible is the story of the evolution of Yahweh. Since Yahweh is a god- image, Yahweh grows as does any other archetypal image. In the Bible, we can trace the growth from a rather tentative, immature Yahweh towards a true and full reflection of the Ultimate. This comes as good news, for it helps us understand the impatient, angry, judgmental Yahweh we frequently meet in the Old Testament.

We can see Yahweh's immaturity in the story of the Garden of Eden. There Yahweh is too fearful to allow humanity to share the tree of the knowledge of good and evil. Similarly, in the story of Noah's flood, Yahweh shows a childish impatience with humans and threatens to destroy them. "God said to Noah, 'I have determined to make an end of all flesh, for the earth is filled with violence because of them; now I am going to destroy them along with the earth'." (Genesis 6:13) There are many more instances of Yahweh's impatience and immaturity, but these two are enough to give us the flavour.

The Bible, then, is the story of the partnership between Yahweh and humanity coming to maturity. Both are bound together in the journey. As one evolves, so does the other. The journey is long and arduous, and fulfilment lies in the mythic future. All the more reason for doing our little part in moving life on.

Reflection questions

1. How has your understanding of God changed since childhood?
2. Does seeing that the biblical God is not the Ultimate God make God more or less real for you?
3. Has monotheism helped or hindered the growth of humanity?

Your thoughts

10
Naming God
(Exodus 3)

"What's in a name?" asked Shakespeare. "A rose by any other name would smell as sweet."[4]

With all due respect to the Bard, I don't think those lines quite express the power of a name. "Rose" for us is not a neutral word. Whenever we hear it, the fragrance and beauty of the flower flood into our memory. A name often expresses or takes on something of the quality or character of its subject.

This was more true in biblical times than in ours. To know a person's name meant knowing something about that person's character. Jacob literally means "one who supplants," and he lived up to his name until his night of wrestling. There he was renamed Israel and became the father of a nation. Such a radical change required a new name.

God needs a name

Even God needs a name, or many names. This is a special challenge since we have the God of the mythic realm and the Ultimate God; not identical but intimately related. They need separate but related names. I will begin with the God of the heavenly or mythic realm, named Yahweh in the Christian tradition.

The biblical account of the naming of Yahweh goes like this. Moses, in the midst of a mystic, mystifying encounter before a burning bush, hurled a question to the demanding presence: "What is your name?" To respond to the call to free his people, Moses needed to hear a name.

The voice answered, "I am who I am" (Exodus 3:14), a form of the verb "to be," now usually translated as Yahweh. (In my younger, King James Version days, it was translated Jehovah, a name which still evokes in me a sense of awesome, fearful, holiness.) "To be" is to exist, to have reality. This name must have conveyed to Moses and the Hebrews a sense of the Reality that is the source of their being. Under this name, they were prepared to follow Moses, sometimes reluctantly, out of Egypt and into the wilderness.

A NRSV footnote to the biblical passage adds that Yahweh can also be translated as, "I am what I am" or "I will be what I will be." In light of this latter possibility, perhaps it would not be totally inaccurate to say that Yahweh means "I am always becoming." Which means that no name can ever be final or complete.

Since ours is "a time of the changing of the gods" — to quote the opening words of the movie *Hawaii* — we welcome such open-endedness. Something happening in the human psyche is being reflected in the way we understand divinity. New names are being born.

Having made the leap of seeing Yahweh as a god-image — the vision of the Ultimate that emerged in the mythic mind of the Hebrew people — we can imagine Yahweh and the Ultimate intimately intertwined. The poet William Blake defines "the Jehovah [Yahweh] of the Bible being no other than he who dwells in flaming fire"[5], and that fire is the Mystery seeking to find expression. Yahweh, then, is created by the tension of the Ultimate fire desiring to commune with the Hebrew people.

Eros: the essence of our nature

Yahweh is also created by our desire to commune with the Ultimate. The naming of Yahweh tells us something of our own nature and, because we reflect divinity, the nature and hence the name of the Ultimate. Divinity must be the cosmic reality of the essence of our own nature. What is that essence or quality?

I believe that the most common, fundamental and continuous experience of life is yearning, wanting, desiring — a passion for life. We are yearning creatures. From the moment of birth until the time we die, we want, we desire, we long for. We want our physical needs met. We yearn for emotional connection. We desire sexual union. We long for love. We want to know, to grow, to become. We want our lives to have meaning and purpose. We yearn for connection with the ultimate. And on and on.

For me, the Greek word eros best sums up this thirst for life.

We tend to equate the erotic with sexual desire, but it goes far beyond that to include all our wanting. Eros is the passionate energy within us reaching out for life.

The whole universe shares our Eros nature. Creation is the garden of Eros. Every atom yearns for every other atom. After the Big Bang blew it all apart, everything wants to come together again, and it keeps happening. Atoms are continually coming together in ever more complex ways, humans being merely the most complex we know about. Every stone, star, tree and animal lives within a great web of yearning. Every rock, in its own way, wants to be a mountain. Every acorn yearns to be an oak. Each one of us, if the yearning has not been squeezed out of us, wants to become the most and best we can be.

God is Eros

This elemental quality, the source and energy of everything, must reflect what we can know of the nature of the Ultimate Mystery. A yearning universe reflects a yearning God. God is Eros: the passionate, yearning, creating energy that throbs in, through, and behind everything.

Since "Eros" is a Greek word for love, we can echo the age-old message that God is love, and love makes the world go round.

The New Testament affirms that "God is love" (1 John 4:16b). However, the word used is not *eros* but *agape*. Agape is a good word, for it expresses the love that focuses on the welfare of the other. God's love (agape) focuses on our welfare. Nothing we can do, however terrible, will cut us off from this love — a valuable message.

I believe, however, that Eros includes this quality. Eros is forever and always at work in us and in everything, and nothing we do can change that. (That does not mean we can't warp it and even turn it demonic, but Eros will always be there).

Agape seems rather one-sided, while Eros requires mutuality. Agape does not need love to be returned, but Eros is a relationship. Within agape, God can become distant and unaffected by what we do. With Eros, our attitude and actions matter profoundly to God. As we awaken to our mutuality with God, I believe Eros more adequately expresses our experience of the Ultimate.

Naming God as Eros means accepting ourselves as erotic creatures reflecting the nature of the Ultimate Mystery. As such, we can have moments and seasons of fulfilment, but we will never be fully satisfied until we become true lovers of God, and all that reflects God — which is me, you, the whole of humanity, and the entire universe.

Our god-image, Yahweh, is our mythic companion on the journey. Yahweh acts like a buffer or transformer that mediates the burning desire of pure Eros through an image that shows us as much of divinity as we can face at any particular moment. Yahweh grows as we grow. We grow as Yahweh grows. The goal for both is always to become true embodiments of Eros.

A more profound meaning for our lives I can't imagine!

Reflection questions

1. What meaning has been in your naming of children, partners, pets, boats, etc.?
2. What is the central or primary yearning in your life?
3. How would you describe your role in bringing God to wholeness?

Your thoughts

11
Born from above
(John 3; Psalm 139; Jeremiah 1)

The fundamentalists are right. You must be born again!

No doubt you've met up with some zealous Christian who has confronted you with the question "Are you saved?" and/or "Are you born again?" My answer is simply to say, "Yes," even though what I mean by that differs radically from what they seem to mean.

They are, of course, referring to the passage in John's gospel where Jesus tells Nicodemus that he must be "born again" (John 3:3); or born "from above," or "anew," depending on which translation you use. I prefer "born from above." It fits my framework of belief, just as "born again" does for a fundamentalist.

My short explanation is that our true selves must be born within us or we will not be who we were born to be. When that happens, we are born anew and "saved."

A confusing question

To think of being born from above, or again, is still strange imagery. Nicodemus can be forgiven for being bewildered. His response was, "Can one enter a second time into the mother's womb and be born?" (John 3:4) We are with him. We more easily think of being physically born and then growing and developing without reference to any further births! We understand that there are different ages and stages as we move through life, and many theories and books can enlighten us to our benefit. Yet we remain as confused as Nicodemus in understanding being born *again.*

However, in the light of our three-reality universe, the idea of being born from above can add another dimension of meaning for us. If you are like me, you have an awareness of a "me" within me struggling to be alive and real within the world. There is a self or soul in there, or somewhere, that wants to become real in the world. It is something more than my physical/emotional/rational self. It is my truth, the essence and purpose of my life.

What is this elusive self? Where does it come from? Where does it reside?

We are probing a great mystery here. There are no definite or complete answers, but I believe that the self resides in the mythic, or heavenly, realm.

Remember the three dimensions of reality: the everyday historic/psychic realm, the mythic/heaven realm, and the Ultimate God/Eros/Oneness realm. The here-and-now realm is where the rubber hits the road. Life happens in our here-and-now world. I must live, and be whoever I'm going to be, in this world of flesh and stone. But my "self," the essence and possibility of who I am, is born and lives in another realm.

We can imagine the yearning of God feeling the need for some bit of work to be done in the historic realm and creating a self or soul to carry it out. To put it more crudely, God looks down (or up, or over, or in, or out), sees a baby being born, and says, "I have a job for you."

We hear this theme in the call of Jeremiah, who hears God say, "Before I formed you in the womb I knew you, and before you were born I consecrated you; I appointed you a prophet to the nations." (Jeremiah 1:5)

The Psalmist says, similarly, "For it was you [Yahweh] who formed my inward parts; you knit me together in my mother's womb. . . . when I was being made in secret, intricately woven in the depths of the earth. Your eyes beheld my unformed substance. In your book were written all the days that were formed for me, when none of them as yet existed." (Psalm 139:13,15-16) I don't believe this means that all the notes of our lives are all dictated by some higher power, and we merely play the record. It does mean, however, that there is a purpose, which may include many interests and activities, for each of us. Whether we find that purpose and live it is another question.

Living our true purpose

Thus the essence of who we are, our soul or self, our place in the big scene, may be alive in the heavenly realm even before we are born! We are born as the vehicle that can embody our purpose within the world, but discovering and living that purpose takes a lifetime. We are created with the receiving apparatus, but tuning in requires careful attention and listening.

We do not automatically know ourselves or our purpose in the world. That knowledge dwells in the elusive mystery of the heavenly realm. All the problems and possibilities of communing with that level of reality come into play. Through outward events and circumstances and inner promptings, we become aware of what calls and nourishes us. Some will have one single purpose, others may have a whole range of interests that bring satisfaction and fulfilment. And the focus may change over time.

As life moves on, we catch glimpses, have moments of insight, which gradually reveal to us the course of our lives. Sometimes, like Paul on the Damascus road, a grand flash of revelation tells us who we are. Many have to wrestle long and hard, like Jacob at the Jabbock river. But however it happens, new birth describes it well. As we come home to ourselves, flesh and spirit come together, heaven and earth are wed, our truth and tasks are united with our gifts and potential.

Challenge and reward

As humanity struggles toward maturity, or as the yearning of Eros evolves a true partner, much remains to be done. Humanity has a long way to go. We are each given a little part toward getting there, which first takes shape as a "self" in the mythic realm. This "self" must be born into a physical life and live in the world. Then, to the degree that we live authentically, we return to the mythic realm and add to the growing universal consciousness. In this way, our lives become part of the mix from which new selves are born to carry on the task of a growing humanity.

There is many a slip 'twixt the cup and the lip. It is not as easy as it sounds. The forces arrayed against our spiritual birth are many and powerful.

However, the reward of being fully alive, of doing what we are here to do, is profound fulfilment and satisfaction. Our souls are awakened, our senses enlivened, our spiritual and physical selves united. To quote the Psalmist, "Such knowledge is too wonderful for me; it is so high that I cannot attain it." (Psalm 139:6)

    When asked "Are you saved?" we can respond with a resounding "Yes."

Reflection questions

1. Are you aware of a "you" within you who struggles to be fully present in the world?
2. Do you resonate with the biblical idea that your "self," or purpose in life, comes from "above"?
3. We both know and don't know our deepest selves. How does this statement relate to your life?

Your thoughts

12
The rainbow covenant
(Genesis 6:5-9:17)

Yahweh was in a major snit.

Humanity was not shaping up according to Yahweh's expectations. What a frustrating and disheartening lot these humans were. The whole idea of creating them in God's image was not working out. Whatever they were supposed to be and do was not happening, at least not to Yahweh's satisfaction: "Every inclination of the thoughts of their hearts was only evil continually." (Genesis 6:5b)

Yahweh was experiencing the common human problem of not understanding why people (partners, minorities, different cultures, etc.) do not shape up the way we think they should. Yahweh — as often happens to us — could not cope with free, independent creatures who insist on going their own way, even when they really don't know what they are doing and end up doing terrible things. Yahweh wanted to pull the plug before matters got totally out of hand.

"So the Lord said, 'I will blot out from the earth the human beings I have created — people together with animals and creeping things and birds of the air, for I am sorry that I have made them'." (Genesis 6:7)

But Yahweh made one exception: "Noah found favor in the sight of the Lord." (Genesis 6:8) Yahweh really wanted humans to become what they were supposed to be and saw in Noah a glimmer of possibility. So Yahweh said to him, "I have seen that you alone are righteous before me in this generation." (Genesis 7:1b)

Build an ark

Yahweh confided to Noah, "I have determined to make an end of all flesh . . . [so] make yourself an ark." (Genesis 6:13a,14a) Noah did, and the legend of Noah and the flood is still among the most familiar of biblical stories. (The story belongs to a tradition of flood stories coming out of the Tigris-Euphrates valley. Tradition and archaeological evidence both confirm that there was a some kind of a great flood, but the biblical writers use it for their own purposes.)

Noah rounded up all the living creatures, two by two (or in part of the account, seven pairs of the clean animals — two traditions are combined in the one account), and herded them into the ark.

It rained for forty days and forty nights, "and all flesh died that moved on the earth." (Genesis 7:21) "And the waters swelled on the earth for one hundred fifty days. But God remembered Noah." (Genesis 7:24-8:1) It sounds as if Noah was not at the top of Yahweh's list of concerns; but, when Noah and the ark did flick back into Yahweh's mind, Yahweh did pay attention, dried up the earth, and made it habitable again.

Noah, with his wife, his three sons and their wives, and all the living creatures, then disembarked from the ark. In thanksgiving "Noah built an altar to the Lord . . . and offered burnt offering on the altar." (Genesis 8:20)

A shocked Yahweh

Perhaps it was Noah's offering, or all the death and carnage, or simply the impact of the whole experience, that shocked Yahweh into realizing the awfulness of what had happened. Edgar Allan Poe put it well when he said, "Each man kills the thing he loves." Yahweh very nearly did the same thing. We tend to project onto our beloved the perfection we do not possess, and then become angry at them when they do not measure up to it. This seems to have happened between Yahweh and humanity.

Fortunately there is more to Yahweh than destructive impulses. Suddenly Yahweh realized that destroying humanity was not the answer. No matter how foolish, these human creatures must be allowed to make their own way. Yahweh had to take their freedom and independence seriously — a lesson that most of us are still in the process of learning!

The covenant

Yahweh, at least for the moment, learned from the experience and responded with the great promise: "I will never again curse the ground because of humankind . . . nor will I ever again destroy every living creature as I have done. As long as the earth endures, seedtime and harvest, cold and heat, summer and winter, day and night, shall not cease." (Genesis 8:21-22)

As an abiding symbol of this covenant, Yahweh added, "I have set my bow in the clouds, and it shall be a sign of the covenant between me and the earth." (Genesis 9:13) So we have the rainbow covenant.

Any covenant involves commitments by both parties. This one, however, fails to spell out the responsibilities of the human partner. We can assume, however, that commitments are involved. Yahweh has committed to preserving humanity and the earth, but this covenant cannot be kept unless we (humanity) do our part. We are Yahweh's head and hands. If we abuse the earth, we can annul the covenant.

The earth is not ours to use as we will. It, and every creature upon it, must be allowed the integrity of its own life. Yes, the earth exists for our good, but only in the same way that we exist for the earth's good. Gandhi said that "the earth can support our need but not our greed."

As those who bring consciousness to the earth, we need to help, as we can, the earth and all her creatures to experience the fullness of life. Our focus must include not only ourselves, but must also broaden to encompass the earth, the universe, and God.

Bodies of the earth

In case this sounds too abstract, too far removed from everyday reality, remember that our bodies, being made of clay, represent our most intimate relationship with the earth. We share with this earth the very molecules that form our bodies. We will tend to regard the earth as we do our bodies. Do we honour and respect our bodies? Do we properly nourish and take care of our bodies? Do we take pleasure in our bodies? Do we appropriately pleasure and take pleasure in others' bodies? Do we practice the necessary disciplines (eating, exercise, sex, quietness, aloneness, togetherness, etc.) that will nourish our own bodies and enhance others'?

As Paul asked, "Do you not know that you are God's temple?" (1 Corinthians 3:16)

Next time you see a rainbow, think upon these things. The rainbow contains the whole spectrum of colour, a great symbol for the wholeness and joy that grow from mutual respect and enrichment. You don't, however, have to wait for a rainbow to make it the attitude of your life.

Reflection questions

1. What ways in which we mistreat our environment especially bother you?
2. How can we help ourselves and our society understand our relationship to the earth as a covenant?
3. What do you learn about Yahweh in the flood story?

Your thoughts

13
From Jacob to Israel
(Genesis 25:19-33:20)

The biblical pattern for discovering and accepting one's purpose or destiny is laid down in the story of Jacob. From Genesis 25:19 to 33:20, the drama unfolds. It sounds like history but is more a mythic, archetypal tale arising out of the memory and hope of the Hebrew people.

Let's look at it.

Jacob, the supplanter

Jacob is an unsavoury character, a devious, greedy, grasping man who took what he could get by any means possible. We love him, for most of us also have a streak of the devious within us.

Jacob's character is clear right from the first. Born grasping his brother Esau's heel, he wants to take his brother's place and claim the status of firstborn. Appropriately, they name him Jacob, which means one who supplants.

He does so by stealing both Esau's birthright and blessing, which represent the family possessions and the role or destiny passed on to the eldest son.

The birthright is easy. Jacob catches Esau at a weak moment. Returning from the fields tired and hungry, Esau smells Jacob's delicious stew as it cooks over the fire and asks for some, for "he was famished." Jacob sees his chance and says, "First sell me your birthright." Esau, a rough outdoors type not big on delayed gratification, accepts: "I am about to die; of what use is a birthright to me?" (Genesis 25:29-34)

Stealing Esau's blessing presents a bigger challenge. In a carefully contrived plot concocted by his mother Rebekah — Jacob came by his deviousness honestly! — Jacob manages to fool his blind father Isaac into thinking he is Esau. Isaac, believing his eldest son is before him, confers the blessing on Jacob.

"Now Esau hated Jacob because of the blessing." (Genesis

27:41) Once again, brother threatens to kill brother. But, with the help of his mother, Jacob escapes to Haran, her ancestral home.

Strange encounter

Jacob stops for the night at Bethel and there has a strange encounter with the Holy. You've all sung "We are Climbing Jacob's Ladder." Beyond the image of the ladder, the song has nothing to do with the original story, but Jacob does see a ladder, "and the angels of God were ascending and descending on it." (Genesis 28:12b)

In his dream, Jacob hears a voice repeating the original promise to Abraham and Sarah: "I am the Lord, the God of Abraham your father . . . The land on which you lie I will give to you and to your offspring . . . and all the families of the earth shall be blessed in you and in your offspring." There is an added assurance: "Know that I am with you and will keep you wherever you go, and will bring you back to this land." (Genesis 28:13-15)

The Bible frequently offends our notion that God ought to bless only good people. Jacob, the devious cheat, is touched by God. The birthright and blessing come with a profound responsibility. A deep call to carry the destiny of Israel is stirring, but, at this point, Jacob pays little attention.

Life goes on

Jacob proceeds to Haran. There, in a touching and dramatic scene by the watering well, he meets and instantly falls in love with his cousin, Rachel. He must, however, work seven years for Rachel's hand; "and they seemed to him but a few days because of the love he had for her." (Genesis 29:20)

But at the wedding, wily uncle Laban, Rachel's father, pawns off on Jacob Rachel's older sister, Leah.

Jacob gets Rachel a week later (there being no one-wife limit in those days), but only after promising to work for Laban another seven years. Leah, the unloved but fertile wife, and Rachel, the loved but barren wife, along with their maids and the children, form a household with all kinds of interesting, funny, and very dysfunctional family dynamics.

Jacob, whose job is to tend Laban's flocks, eventually outmanoeuvres his employer and ends up with most of the herd as his pay. This makes him *persona non grata;* so much so that he has to leave with his wives, children, maids (who also have children by him!) and all his ill-gotten animals.

But where will he go? Again Jacob hears THE VOICE. "Return to the land of your ancestors and to your kindred, and I will be with you." (Genesis 31:3)

Returning home seems like a great idea, but with one little problem. It means meeting Esau, who, at last report, wanted to kill him.

The crunch comes

The crunch comes on the banks of the Jabbock river. Jacob can't go back because an angry Laban is there. Across the river is Esau. Jacob sends out spies who inform him that   Esau is approaching with four hundred men.

Jacob prays, "Deliver me, please, from the hand of my brother . . . for I am afraid of him; he may come and kill us all. . . Yet you have said, 'I will surely do you good'" (Genesis 32:11-12) Jacob is caught between fear and promise. Ever the schemer, he sends his wives, maids, flocks, and herds across the river, with the hope of appeasing Esau.

Then comes the famous night of wrestling: "Jacob was left alone; and a man wrestled with him until daybreak." (Genesis 32:24) Was the man his conscience, the evil one, or God? Probably all three.

Transformation

Jacob is put to the wall. His chickens have come home to roost. He must face himself and the results of his duplicity. As the night wears on, and he purges the depths of his being, he hears the man say, "You shall no longer be called Jacob, but Israel, for you have striven with God and with humans, and have prevailed." (Genesis 32:28)

Something profound is going on. Change is happening. Out of the crucible of his wrestling Jacob, the supplanter, becomes Israel, the father of a nation. He finds his true self and his destiny. He becomes the servant of the promise, and spends the rest of his life being the father of a nation.

This pattern is repeated again and again, in one way or another, throughout the Bible and in countless lives. If we, like Jacob, faithfully wrestle, the destiny of our lives will be born in us.

Reflection questions

1. Think of a time of inner wrestling, and what it meant for your life.
2. With what person, or persons, in the story do you identify, and why?
3. How would you describe Jacob's morality and what it means for us?

Your thoughts

14
Be a blessing
(Genesis 12:1-9)

"I am blessed." Have you said that? Have you heard others say it? What did you (they) mean?

When I say it, I am referring to some especially good aspect of life. I feel satisfied, fulfilled, whole. I say it of my present marriage, which is most fulfilling and life-enhancing. I am blessed with five children who are of the essence of my life. Three step-children and a couple of grandchildren add to the blessing. The list could go on to home, and work, and now retirement, all great blessings.

Blessing is life

"Blessing" is anything that gives life depth, richness, and purpose. The Old Testament talks about blessing in connection with family, herds, possessions, and all the good things of life. To be blessed is to be smiled upon by God, of which the immediate evidence is those people and possessions that bring a joyous exuberance and inner wholeness to our lives.

"Blessing" is at the heart of the promise to Abram and Sarai (whose names are later changed to the more familiar Abraham and Sarah). In an early scene (Genesis 12), we meet the theme of the Bible.

Life presented Abram and Sarai with an open moment. They had to move to another place, and the world and the future lay before them. Already, instigated by Abram's father, Terah, they had come up the Tigris-Euphrates valley from Ur and were in Haran. As Bedouin shepherds searching for pasture on the edge of more settled centres, they were vulnerable to the caprice of nature and to population shifts. An influx of settlers from the north (about 2,000 BCE) had necessitated the first move, but now Haran was also becoming crowded. Where would they go?

"Now the Lord said to Abram [Yahweh, a patriarchal male

God, tended to speak primarily to the male patriarchs!], 'Go from your country and your kindred and your father's house to the land that I will show you. I will make of you a great nation, and I will bless you, and make your name great, so that you will be a blessing. I will bless those who bless you, and the one who curses you I will curse; and in you all the families of the earth shall be blessed.'. . . And they set forth to go to the land of Canaan." (Genesis 12:1-5b)

A mythic memory

This account is no doubt the result of later generations reading meaning back into the stories of their ancestors. It may often be a case of remembering things that never happened! We must, however, also remember that these stories do have a basis in history. Populations did move and the Hebrew people did emerge.

This mythic memory represents a happening within the psyche of the Hebrew people that awakened them to the purpose of their existence. Ever after, the vision of this promise shaped them and pulled them forward as much as they were pushed by the movement of history. This noble intuition sent them on their way to search out through the vagaries of their history just how they could accomplish being a blessing.

We, whether as Christians or members of western culture, inherit this promise. As individuals, as countries, corporations, or any group of people, we need to understand that our purpose in life is to bring blessing. We don't always act on this insight, and often our vision is very narrow, but in there somewhere we must agree that life is about blessing, for "in you all the families of the earth shall be blest." (Genesis 12:3b)

Whatever your particular gift or purpose, you can bring blessing. Everything you are and do should enrich life. Every individual, every country, every business, every organization, every religion must answer the question of blessing. How are you a blessing?

Be someone

The promise to Abram and Sarai gives some clues as to how we can go about being a blessing. The first part of the promise is, "I will make of you a great nation." (Genesis 12:2a) To be a blessing, you must first be somebody. In order to give of ourselves, we must possess ourselves. This is a lifetime work.

Our adolescence is a special time of gathering together the degree of self-possession necessary to leave behind our childhood, our dependent time, and make our own way in the world. We then explore, develop relationships, become educated, develop skills and a degree of maturity that enables us to establish ourselves in life. We now have something to give, though the learning goes on throughout our lives.

The second part of the promise is "I will bless you. . . so that you will be a blessing." (Genesis 12:2b) To be a blessing, you must allow your blessings to nourish you.

You've heard of mixed blessings — ones that have a downside as well as an upside. Most things in life are like that. We must strive to make our blessings as rich and full as possible. If aspects of life drain our energy and creativity, we must deal with them. Childhood is our original blessing. We must accept it and draw from it, even if it was horrendous. Work is usually ambivalent; some aspects of it nourish us, and others simply drain us. We must focus on the good or find a better situation. Marriage can be bane or blessing. Having painfully decided to end my first marriage, I know that sometimes that is the route to blessing, but only as a last resort.

Be a blessing

The bottom line is, "In you all the families of the earth shall be blessed." (Genesis 12:3b) We are here to serve, to offer what we can to the human good.

Our vision may be too small, too narrow, too self-centred, and we stop short of our potential. Politicians exercise power for the select few. Corporations stop at the bottom line. Religions serve themselves rather than the world. As individuals, we focus on ourselves and our own small circle.

The challenge to bless is always before us. Therefore, be a blessing.

Reflection questions

1. Count your blessings.
2. How can we speak of blessing in the face of the terrible injustices within our world?
3. To whom, and how, are you a blessing?

Your thoughts

15
Leaving home
(Exodus, Judges)

You will remember, or perhaps you are in the midst of, that time when in the eyes of your teenager you suddenly ceased to know anything and became a total embarrassment. Actually, your children were right on track. Life was proceeding as it should. They were leaving home. They were developing the psychic distance necessary to become persons in their own right.

The Exodus as personal and political

In the story of the Hebrew people, that's one way to read the Exodus. Their escape from slavery in Egypt is the adolescent stage of our personal journey, something we all must make.

At another level, the Exodus is a political story and can be read as the struggle of every oppressed people to gain their freedom. Any person or group who must deal with oppression of any kind (in the family, at work, within organized religion, in relation to governments, and anywhere it occurs) can find hope here. In this light, it has given heart and courage to many facing discrimination, abuse, torture, and even death.

Every nation, every person, every society, every family, every organization must go through some sort of similar process. As individuals and as peoples, we must gain the strength and resolve to establish ourselves and take our rightful place, which is what the Exodus did for the Hebrews. Some psychologists call this process "differentiation."

In the face of the grandeur of the Exodus story as a symbol of the struggle for freedom, reading it as an account of our personal growth may seem petty and trite. It does apply, however, to both the personal and the political. And if we are to offer anything toward bringing justice and wholeness to the world, we must do our own inner work as well as confront the external powers of darkness.

In the realm of personal journey, I read the Exodus as the natural unfolding of life, with special relevance for our adolescence. That is the time when hormones awaken us, and the mystery of sexuality takes on a new and powerful urgency. We find ourselves looking with excitement and terror at an adult world. All the possibilities of life are before us. The big world beckons, and we must try our wings.

"Leaving home" is not only a teenage experience. It keeps happening. Sometimes we must take on a new job, a new marriage. Old belief systems die, and new ones must evolve. Sometimes new attitudes and behaviours must be tried. Just as we are settled into one stage of life, the next one is upon us. Life keeps forcing our hand.

A new king arises

For the Hebrews, trouble began when "a new king arose over Egypt, who did not know Joseph." (Exodus 1:8) Joseph had saved his people in a time of famine by getting them into Egypt. There they prospered under the paternal eye of friendly Pharaohs, but with a new dynasty their situation changed from privilege to slavery.

Isn't that the way life goes? Things roll along fine, and then something happens. It may be in the world or the people around us, or within ourselves, but gradually or suddenly we become aware that we are in some kind of slavery or oppression. At the political level, every indigenous people has found itself enslaved by the nation who entered their country. For the teenager, the warm, secure world of childhood and home becomes a prison, or at best a place that must be left behind.

Among the Hebrews, Moses emerged as the great leader. In any situation, leaders will appear who provide vision, courage, and practical strategies.

In our own lives, we must find and develop our inner leader, the will and courage that can make the decisions and take the needed steps to move forward. We may call it the Intuitive Self or the Christ within, or whatever we name that part of us that attunes to our soul's need and follows it.

Leaving home is not easy. Many forces within us and around

us encourage us to stay. In some people, the stay-put forces are so dominant, or the inner leader so weak, that they never do leave home; most of us have at times chosen to stay with the enslaving old rather than risk the unknown new. Hanging on to a religious belief system that has died is just one example. Our inner leader needs to have courage and be insistent. Moses' cry (Exodus 5:1) to the Pharaoh, "Let my people go," was very insistent.

Mustering our forces

First Moses had to get the people on side. "They would not listen to Moses, because of their broken spirit and their cruel slavery." (Exodus 6:9) Nourishing the vision and courage to carry on the struggle in the face of "cruel slavery" is very daunting. Dictators know the power of intimidation and torture, and dictators abound not only in countries but in institutions, organizations, even in our homes — and especially in our heads.

Dealing with oppressing forces requires all the wisdom, strategy, patience, and boldness we can muster. Moses had a major struggle with the Pharaoh. Again and again, he and his brother Aaron warned the Pharaoh of a coming plague if he did not "let my people go." The Pharaoh's reluctance may have been because all the plagues were more or less the natural disasters of the country, but with the death of every firstborn in the land, he finally relented.

The Hebrews then took the great step into freedom, but before them was the wilderness.

Facing the wilderness

A wilderness always awaits. All those alluring possibilities are uncharted territory filled with decisions and challenges. Our internal leader needs strength and courage to withstand the pressures and enable us to take responsibility for ourselves. Many of the Hebrews died in the wilderness. Even if we don't physically die, we may do so as far as creative growth and following our soul's path is concerned. And many people have died facing the real oppressors of this world.

It took them forty years (about the time it takes us), but eventually the Hebrews made it to the promised land. They entered it in either one great blitz (Joshua's version) or a little bit at a time, and never completely (Judges).

The second version fits most of us. We get our act together a little bit at a time, and never completely. For oppressed peoples, gaining freedom is a long, slow, hard, and dangerous struggle. Through it all, the vision of the promised land keeps hope alive. The possibility of a better life and a more just and loving world spurs us on.

When we enter the promised land, for a moment or for a season, we know that "leaving home" and facing the wilderness was well worth the venture.

Reflection questions

1. Think upon your adolescent experience of "leaving home" and venturing into life. What are your strongest memories?
2. What do you know of situations where "exodus" is an empowering vision for those oppressed by vicious totalitarian regimes?
3. How has your life been shaped by times you have left the old (work, belief, marriage, etc.) and ventured on a new path?

Your thoughts

16
Making our mark
(1 Samuel, 2 Chronicles)

We may believe that we have control over our lives, but I think we often make our choices within a narrower range than we imagine. Sometimes our genes and the flow of life dictate that certain things will happen.

Like other nations

So it was with the Hebrew people. There came a point when they wanted "a king to govern [them], like other nations." (1 Samuel 8:5b)

The political situation was chaotic. Since entering the "promised land" several generations before, they had been more or less ruled by a series of charismatic leaders called "judges." These were local leaders who had a very tenuous hold over the whole area settled by the twelve tribes of Israel.

The Philistines, who arrived after the Hebrews and who were more technologically advanced, had considerable success in wrestling major portions of the country from them. To survive, the Hebrews needed a central authority to muster their allegiance and organize them.

Samuel, the "judge" at the time, was getting old and had no apparent successor. This led the elders to conclude that they must have a king. Two accounts, one in favour of the kingship and one against, are woven together, but we can well imagine that both schools existed.

The dangers of kingship

Samuel saw the kingship as an affront to Yahweh. The people had supposedly chosen Yahweh as their king. Choosing a human king would undermine their dependence on Yahweh. Yahweh, a step ahead of Samuel on this one, agreed but knew that the people would have their way; the situation demanded it. So Yahweh told

Samuel, "listen to their voice; only — you shall solemnly warn them, and show them the ways of the king who shall reign over them. (1 Samuel 8:9)

Samuel reported the words of Yahweh to the people. He warned them that the king "will take your sons . . . . your daughters . . . . the best of your fields and vineyards." (1 Samuel 8:9-14) In other words, taxes were coming. "But the people refused to listen," (1 Samuel 8:19) and insisted on having a king.

Then unfold the fascinating accounts of Saul, David, and Solomon, the three kings who created a nation and held it together for a time.

The Hebrews never did become a superpower. But in a time when the Egyptians and Babylonians, the great powers which sandwiched them on either side, were in decline, they briefly became a power to be reckoned with. A few centuries later, that status would come to a disastrous end, but they did have their moment in the sun.

In becoming a nation, the Hebrews met needs no different from those of any other group of people. In order to live out our purpose, we need to be recognized as a distinct people (a fact that needs recognition within the Canadian context). The struggles of indigenous people, and many minorities, testify to the need of people to have control over their own destiny. How we can manage to be distinct peoples and yet one human family is the political agenda.

A model for our individual journeys

Israel becoming a nation is also a pattern for our individual journeys. There comes a point when we must take our place in the adult world as the special individuals we are.

We want to make a living, be part of a family or intimate group, and belong to various and sundry communities. Who we are, where we are, our capabilities and limitations are all part of the mix. Through external necessity and internal, often unconscious, forces, we will make a life for ourselves.

For the majority of us, but not all, there comes a time for choosing a partner. The yearning for a partner seems to be written into our genes and in the morphogenetic fields that mould us. When the forces kick in, they are deeper than our will. Even as those opposing the kingship had no power to stop it, the part of us that may protest ultimately carries little weight. We will often make a bad marriage rather than no marriage.

Parenting, with or without a partner, is often another major urge of adult life. The human race wants to continue. We now have more choice in this area, but often there emerges a powerful yearning, much deeper than our rational minds, that must be dealt with. Parenting, either as biological parents, extended family, or community service, remains one of the primary works of adult life that gives us identity and meaning — and a sense of immortality.

Work, career, or doing something in the world, remains a major focus of adult life. We are pushed on by the necessity of making a living, but often our paid work is only part of what we do in the world. Our most important ways of expressing ourselves and making a contribution can be in our homes, our hobbies, and our volunteer work. However we do it, we want to leave our mark.

The urge to form communities lies deeply within us. We live life within communities: geographical, social, religious, political, etc. And with communities comes the desire and responsibility for leading and maintaining them.

Partnering, parenting, work, and community are the pillars of our adult life energies. Many of us participate in all of them; some manage (and are often content with) one or two.

All in all, most of us, in our twenties and thirties, take a crack at being as other people and taking our place in the adult world.

Be warned

Be warned. Dangers await. Samuel warned the people that the best of their energies would go into maintaining the king and the kingdom. The best of our energies will go into partnering, parenting, work, and community. While these are good things, they impose limits. We can become busy, busy, busy. Those immersed in "career" often have little energy for anything else. Parts of ourselves will not find expression. We will have little time to explore our inner world.

But that's fine. This stage, too, will pass. Life is taking its natural course. When it is your time to "Be as other nations," do it. If you are fortunate, you will find much that is satisfying and fulfilling and you will be carrying on the life and work of the world.

Reflection questions

1. What is your experience of the tension between following your dreams, desires, inner yearnings and callings and being consumed by the responsibilities and busyness of your life?
2. Is there something you really want to do for yourself and for the world?
3. What do you feel is the calling or destiny of your country?

Your thoughts

17
Makers of history
(Isaiah to Malachi)

"Ezekiel saw a wheel a rollin', way in the middle of the air; A wheel within a wheel a rollin', way in the middle of the air." The old camp song gives us some inkling of the magnificence of Ezekiel's vision of divine presence.

Ezekiel was big on visions; right up there with the writers of Daniel, Zechariah, and Revelation. He reports that, "I was among the exiles by the river Chebar, and the heavens were opened, and I saw visions of God." (Ezekiel 1:1) A stormy wind came out of the north. He saw fire and brightness and in the middle were four living creatures. Around them were wheels with eyes all around that move like wheels within wheels and go in all directions. Over this strange carriage is a dome and a throne — but a brief summary cannot do it justice; you really must read it. (Ezekiel 1)

Ezekiel "was among the exiles." (Ezekiel 1:1) The Exile, the most traumatic event of Hebrew history, saw their nation destroyed and many of the people deported to Babylon. It must have seemed like the end. Everything that had given them security and meaning was gone. Their God had utterly failed them. Ezekiel's vision of the divine presence leaving the temple is a poignant and powerful symbol of what he experienced. (Ezekiel 8-10)

Hope from despair

We are, however, creatures of hope: "Weeping may linger for the night, but joy comes with the morning." (Psalm 30:5b) When loss or disaster befalls us we "lie down and bleed a while, then rise and fight again." Often we emerge from a crisis or disaster enlarged and strengthened.

That's what happened with the Hebrew people. Ezekiel's visionary awareness of the overpowering presence of the divine, and then the divine leaving the temple, was a clue that something significant was happening within the psyche of the Hebrew people. A door closed, but another opened. Hope was stirring. A new vision of the divine could now emerge. The disaster of the Exile was drawing them to a new level of consciousness.

This new thrust in human awareness had begun with the eighth century BCE prophets. In Amos, Hosea, Micah and Isaiah (1-39), prophesy reached new heights.

We tend to think of prophesy as foretelling the future. What's going to happen? We all want to know. The prophets were quick to oblige, but they did not simply foretell what was going to happen. Behind their predictions was a big "if." This will happen *if* you do not shape up. They had, at one level, a very simple message: "Do what Yahweh says, or face dire consequences."

The implication of the "if" is fundamentally important. It means that the future does not unfold in some mechanical way but depends on our choices and actions. As free, independent creatures, we have the ability and responsibility to create the future. We are the creators of history.

Not doing well

The prophets were keenly aware that the Hebrews were not doing very well. Disaster loomed unless they made major changes.

Injustice haunted Amos: "Let justice roll down like waters, and righteousness like an ever flowing stream." (Amos 5:24)

Hosea experienced the abiding love of Yahweh. Behind all the rantings and ravings of Yahweh, as reported by the prophets, is a theme of constant love. Out of Hosea's own experience of continuing to love his unfaithful wife, he knew that Yahweh "loves the people of Israel, though they turn to other gods." (Hosea 3:1b)

Yahweh, baffled and frustrated by the Israelites, says "I love them. Why won't they do what I want?" "The more I called them, the more they went from me; they kept sacrificing to the Baals, and offering incense to idols." (Hosea 11:2) Yahweh's characteristic patriarchal response was to become angry, even abusive.

But out of this experience came a moment of insight. In spite of everything, Yahweh's love remained. The anger was a cover-up for love: "I led them with cords of human kindness, with bands of love. I was to them like those who lift infants to their cheeks. I bent down to them and fed them." (Hosea 11:4) "My heart recoils within me; my compassion grows warm and tender. I will not execute my fierce anger; . . . I will not come in wrath." (Hosea 11:8b-9)

Here, in the midst of the immaturity of both Yahweh and the people, came the affirmation that the constant love of Eros is always and eternally present, providing the security to endure and to venture into the unknown.

Responsible and accountable

Humanity was being drawn to a new depth of awareness. Gradually the notion that we are moral creatures responsible for creating our future was dawning. Micah sums up the eighth-century BCE insight by saying, "What does the Lord require of you but to do justice, and to love kindness, and to walk humbly with your God" (Micah 6:8) — still a good guide for life's journey.

The explicit awareness of personal responsibility and accountability emerged in Jeremiah and Ezekiel. Both quote a proverb, "The parents have eaten sour grapes, and the children's teeth are set on edge." (Jeremiah 31:29, Ezekiel 18:2) But now, "All shall die for their own sins; the teeth of everyone who eats sour grapes shall be set on edge" (Jeremiah 31:30); and "This proverb shall no more be used by you in Israel. . . it is only the person who sins that shall die." (Ezekiel 18:3b,4b)

The role, the idea, of the individual reached a new level. It triggered in Jeremiah an ultimate vision of the shift from external authority to moral authority within. "The days are surely coming, says the Lord, when I will make a new covenant with the house of Israel and the house of Judah. . . . I will put my law within them, and I will write it on their hearts." (Jeremiah 31:31,33)

Ezekiel's vision of god within

Ezekiel had a similar insight, visioned as the mythic and mystical glory of Yahweh, which had departed, now returning to the temple. Despair turned to hope. "The vision I saw was like the vision that I had seen . . . by the river Chebar; and I fell upon my face. As the glory of the Lord entered the temple by the gate facing east, the spirit lifted me up, and brought me into the inner court; and the glory of the Lord filled the temple." (Ezekiel 43:3-5)

The vision of Jeremiah and Ezekiel still awaits fulfilment. But the consciousness awakened in them continues to work. We need to come to our own inner temple, where the glory of the divine Self, the self we truly are, fills the temple of our being and radiates out to the world. Only then will we take full responsibility for our world by doing justice, loving compassion, and walking humbly.

Reflection questions

1. Imagine, draw, write about, the vision of God leaving the temple as a metaphor for our society.
2. Where do you see God returning to the temple?
3. When have you made, or failed to make, responsible decisions and how has your life been affected?

Your thoughts

Notes

1. Jean Houston: a mythologist, psychologist, student of sacred traditions, writer, actress (See the Preface and For Further Reading).
2. Mystery School: a creative and wonderful series of nine week-end events, conducted by Jean Houston and her team, exploring the meaning and possibilities of life fashioned on the Greek Mystery School tradition of learning.
3. I owe this insight to Tikva Frymer-Kensky, in her book, *In The Wake of The Goddesses: Women, Culture, and the Biblical Transformation of Pagan Myth*. New York, NY: The Free Press, a Division of Macmillan, Inc., 1992.
4. Shakespeare, William. *Romeo and Juliet,* II, ii, 43
5. Quoted by Edward F. Edinger in *Encounter With The Self,* (Toronto, ON: Inner City Books, 1986), p. 20.

Job

Lament

Ah ....

She walks, through the dark and the dirt
 of the street,
She searches for food for her family to eat.
The soldiers have gone to the corner for beer
She's twelve, so she trembles and walks on in fear.

Oooh..............

Like so many women in present or past
Her needs and her safety and pleasure come last
she grows up to be someone's "woman" or wife,
Her boundaries are set by the men in her life.

Oooh....

We weep for the girl-child and woman out there,
We sing to give birth to a world that is fair.
We struggle for change and a balance of power
Where love and compassion for all come to flower.

FOR WE SHALL LIVE,
AND WE SHALL WALK FREE
JUSTICE BE OUR COMMUNITY!

YES, WE SHALL LIVE,
AND WE SHALL WALK FREE,
JUSTICE BE OUR COMMUNITY!

Emily Kierstead

18
The Blind-siding of Yahweh
(Job)

Do you know what being blind-sided means? It happens to me every now and again. I say or do something stupid or insensitive. Then someone brings it pointedly to my attention, and the painful truth dawns. I wasn't intentionally being a bone head. I was simply blind and unaware. When I'm person enough to admit my guilt, my consciousness grows.

That, according to Carl Jung in *Answer to Job,* is what happened to Yahweh in the book of Job. This dramatic tale tells of Yahweh being blind-sided by Job. Job confronted Yahweh's immoral, or amoral, treatment of him — something no one had dared to do prior to that time. This, Jung believed, precipitated Yahweh's eventual decision to incarnate as a human being.

Job, then, is the pivotal book in the biblical journey. It expresses, through a mythic story, a major happening in the collective unconscious of the Hebrew psyche.

Yahweh tests Job

Let's look at what happened.

The heavenly council (the various sub-personalities of Yahweh), having gathered from their various wanderings, are sitting around commiserating. They recognize Job as a very fine fellow. Satan, however, is not convinced. "Stretch out your hand now, and touch all that he has, and he will curse you to your face." (Job 1:11)

Yahweh gives Satan the green light to do whatever he likes to Job's family and property " only do not stretch out your hand against him!" (Job 1:12) Satan goes gleefully about his task. Calamities befall Job one after another. He loses all his flocks and herds, and even his children.

Through it all, Job stands fast: "In all this Job did not sin or charge God with wrong- doing." (Job 1:22)

There is another heavenly gathering. Satan remains unconvinced of Job's steadfastness. "Stretch out your hand now and touch his bone and his flesh, and he will curse you to your face," Satan says. (Job 2:5)

"Very well," says Yahweh, "he is in your power; only spare his life." (Job 2:6)

Satan inflicts "loathsome sores" (Job 2:7) on Job, who ends up sitting among the ashes scraping himself with a piece of a broken dish. Yet, "in all this Job did not sin with his lips." (Job 2:10) He passed the test.

So ends the prologue of this fine story.

Job responds

The body of the story is a series of dialogues with three "friends": Eliphaz, Bildad and Zophar. A fourth one, Elihu, appears late in the game. In these conversations, we discover that Job is not a docile, sentimental goody-goody.

His friends try to convince him that he must have committed some terrible sin and deserves his ill fate. But Job will have none of it. He knows he is an authentically good person and boldly affirms that he has done nothing to deserve these disasters.

He challenges his so-called friends: "Teach me, and I will be silent; make me understand how I have done wrong." (Job 6:24) "My vindication is at stake. Is there any wrong on my tongue?" (Job 6:29b-30a) "Until I die I will not put away my integrity from me. I hold fast my righteousness, and will not let it go; my heart does not reproach me for any of my days." (Job 27:5b-6)

Yahweh's actions baffle Job. "Your hands fashioned and made me; and now you turn and destroy me," he says (Job 10:8), but he refuses to grovel. He will not be intimidated by Yahweh. He wants to take God on, to argue his case face to face. "I would speak to the Almighty, and I desire to argue my case with God . . . . . I will defend my ways to his face . . . . . I have indeed prepared my case; I know that I shall be vindicated." (Job 13:3,15b,18)

But Yahweh stands aloof. Job searches to no avail. "Oh, that I knew where I might find him, that I might come even to his dwell-

ing! I would lay my case before him . . . [then] he would give heed
to me . . . and I should be acquitted forever by my judge." (Job
23:3-7b)

Job despairs of receiving a fair hearing: "There is no umpire
between us, who might lay his hand on us both." (Job 9:33) He
concludes that Yahweh simply does not understand: "For [Yahweh]
is not a mortal, as I am." (Job 9:32) In his frustration, Job asks
Yahweh, "Do you have eyes of flesh? Do you see as humans see?
Are your days like the days of mortals, or your years like human
years, that you seek out my iniquity? . . . although you know that I
am not guilty." (Job 10:4-7a)

Yahweh learns something new

In the end, tradition wins. Yahweh does appear, but only to over-
whelm Job with bluster and intimidation — four chapters of it
(Job 38-41). An extremely defensive Yahweh shouts, "Will you
even put me in the wrong? Will you condemn me that you may be
justified? Have you an arm like God, and can you thunder with a
voice like [God]?" (Job 40:8-9) Job is forced to admit that, com-
pared to Yahweh's almightiness, he is nothing. In return, Yahweh
restores his fortunes and, supposedly, all is well.

It is a hollow victory. As Jung interprets it, Yahweh has been
severely wounded in the process. No one has ever stood up to
Yahweh as Job has. No one has clung to his integrity as has Job.
No one has ever so forcefully brought to Yahweh's attention the
depths of Yahweh's immorality. Yahweh has done to Job what no
moral person would do to another. Yahweh's behaviour has been
unconscionable.

Yahweh can't blame Satan. Jung draws the obvious to our attention by noting that Satan is not a being apart from Yahweh, but
an aspect of Yahweh. As monotheists we cannot have a dualism,
so evil too must come from Yahweh. Yahweh must take responsibility even for actions perpetrated by Yahweh's dark side, named
Satan.

Yahweh was not being malicious, just blind and unaware.
Yahweh is stung by the accusation that "he is not a mortal." Yahweh
simply does not understand about being human. That Job would

be profoundly offended by what happened to him had not entered Yahweh's consciousness. Yahweh was caught off guard, blind-sided.

Incarnation is the only route

Yahweh faces a momentous decision. Either retreat into aloof lone-liness, as we so often do when confronted by the truth of our-selves. Or enter the human fray by becoming human.

Yahweh, too, has integrity. The divine by nature yearns for wholeness and relationship. The only possibility is to enter history through the life of an individual person.

Thus the yearning for a Messiah is born, one who will live among us with the fullness of divine passion. A door opens that will lead both Yahweh and ourselves to new levels of maturity.

Reflection questions

1. I have suggested that Yahweh learns and grows from experi-ence much as we do. Do you agree, or disagree, and why?
2. Job is the victim of Yahweh's immaturity. Do you ever feel that way? Is there any reality behind it?
3. Job had the will and courage to confront the injustice of Yahweh. What does this tell us about confronting the injus-tice of the world?

Your thoughts

19
Patriarchy
(The Dark Side Of The Biblical Story)

To talk about patriarchy is to enter a minefield, but I'll brave it.

Patriarchy is the social structure of male dominance. For the past five thousand years, give or take a thousand or two, in practically every tribe and culture, it has become woven into the social fabric and resulted in the misuse of male power. Patriarchy is so pervasive that it sinks into the unconscious and becomes part of the accepted structure of our psyches as well as of the social order. We have only begun to note it and uproot it.

As with anything in the unconscious, there have always been hints and flashes of awareness of the demonic aspect of patriarchy. Women have covertly or overtly risen against it in every age. Whether it is the women of Greece threatening to withhold sex if the men continue to go to war[1] or Vashti, the original queen in the story of Esther (which we will look at later) refusing to come to the King's party naked, or the countless women who over the centuries have asserted their strength and uniqueness, resistance has always been there.

Resistance to patriarchy has come in waves or cycles, and is currently reaching a peak. With the powerful emergence of the feminine, an elemental, spiritual force seeks balance and equality between the sexes. We hope that this time it has the strength to bring about a new social order.

My own awakening

All this sounds very cool and rational. In fact, it rarely happens that way. My own awakening happened slowly, sometimes painfully, and continues. It has certainly been a major factor in my own growth and in my rethinking of the Christian tradition.

Becoming aware of how utterly, completely, and drastically women's lives have been warped and shattered by men using and abusing them has been a transforming experience for me. Like

everyone, I have read about these things; I know them at a rational
level. Much deeper awareness has come through listening to women
tell their stories. As a pastoral minister and in my work at
Tatamagouche Centre, I have heard many of these stories. I
companioned one woman into the dark reaches of hell as her memories of childhood abuse gradually came to her. With the help of
good therapists and friends, she came through. But one comes away
from such experiences shaken to the core.

I have also heard some men's stories, sometimes of abuse by
women and sometimes by men. No one is immune.

How did it happen?

How could all this have happened? How could something so monstrous live for so long and we be so blind to it?

Riane Eisler's book, *The Chalice and the Blade*, lays down
the challenge to anyone trying to make sense of human evolution.
Her argument, simply stated, says that long ago, before patriarchy
took over, women were dominant and peace reigned. Towns were
built on plains and had no walls! This blissful scene was shattered
when male-dominated warrior tribes swept down from the north
and took over. Some criticize her for selective scholarship. But, as
Jean Houston says of Eisler, "She may not always be accurate, but
she's true."

Riane Eisler, and many others, makes clear that the Judeo-
Christian tradition, along with the other major religious traditions,
played a major role in the patriarchal takeover, giving it divinely-
sanctioned status.

Deep psychic reasons for patriarchy

Patriarchy arose because of developments within the human psyche.

The inner separation that results from entering consciousness
leaves us with an enormous shadow, or unknown, part of us. What
we don't know we fear. Our complexes and neuroses create the
jails we build within ourselves to keep the unknown at bay. Our
social order and institutions become our communal bastions against
the feared unknown.

For men, the feminine forms a large part of the unknown. She is different from him. He does not understand, and therefore fears, the forces that move in her. But he cannot escape the relentless sexual desire which draws him within her orbit. He must possess her. Yet he fears this awesome power that seems to emanate from her. To protect himself against her and his raging passion he must be cool, rational, unmoved, aloof. He must cut himself off from his own feminine, as well as from the feminine out there.

The typical macho male, out of touch with his feminine side, fears — sometimes with an intensity that can turn to loathing — the softness, gentleness and caring that he identifies with women. He fails to note that his own feminine side is the real source of his fear. He cannot cope with any hint of the feminine within himself. What he cannot accept within himself he projects onto others, in this case onto women. He finds it much easier to blame her rather than look within himself. In the Garden of Eden myth, Adam blamed Eve, and the game has been going on ever since.

So patriarchy believes that women must be controlled, put down, kept down, belittled, degraded, abused, burned at the stake — whatever it takes to keep the power of the feminine at bay.

Patriarchy becomes a pathology

One expression of this pathology is homophobia. Our macho male dare not bring to consciousness any twinge of sexual desire for another male. He projects his deep-rooted fear onto those who are, or are thought to be, homosexual. Hence we have gay bashing, one form of which seizes upon the homophobia of the biblical age to declare that God hates homosexuality. Recognizing and accepting the validity and reality of lesbianism and homosexuality helps break the grip of patriarchy and the homophobia which accompanies it.

Repentance means admitting what actually happened and continues to happen, and then changing direction. Until we men acknowledge the ages of oppression and take responsibility for the present situation, we are not likely to change. I am only beginning to become aware of how widespread and vast were the numbers of women killed in the witch-burning time. Most men are only beginning to comprehend the monstrous oppression visited upon women and how much of that dark shadow continues. And the church, although making some progress, continues to be a bastion of male dominance.

However we see it, the time has come to exorcize patriarchy from our psychic and social reality. Let us get on with it.

✧ ✧ ✧

Reflection questions

1. What is your experience of patriarchy?
2. How does patriarchy continue to affect your work place, church, and home?
3. What is the level of gay/lesbian acceptance in your social circles?

Your thoughts

20
A necessary evil?
(Further Delving Into Patriarchy)

Emily just rolled her eyes heavenward when I mentioned I had
some good things to say about patriarchy; she then went on for a
good while describing its ravages. We men need to understand
that, as women, you carry in your bones the degradation and
suffering endured through five thousand years of male dominance. If, at times, you respond from an elemental, archetypal
reservoir of grief and rage, we men should not be surprised.

I do not want in any way to condone the horrors of patriarchy. I do, however, need to say that, if it had not been patriarchy,
our dark, shadow side would have invented some other monstrous psychic and social structure to be the school for our growing. In that sense, I believe that patriarchy was a necessary evil
on the road to our becoming whole.

Biological basics

First of all, patriarchy has some biological underpinnings. It's
impossible to totally sort out what's social conditioning and what's
biology. Since there are arguments on both sides, there must be a
bit of both. It's also dangerous naming certain qualities masculine and others feminine, yet here too there is some biological
reality. We must also remember that we all carry within ourselves
both the feminine and masculine.

To be brief, I'll say that the feminine centres around nurturing and the masculine around aggression. The woman bears and
nurses the child, the womb and the breast being her unique nurturing sources. The symbol of the male is the flashing sword and
erect penis, ready to fight off other suitors and to impregnate the
woman.

Let me steal a page from Ken Wilber's *A Brief History of
Everything*, in which he talks about male and female hormones.
The female hormone is oxytocin, which "is the 'relationship

drug'; it induces incredibly strong feelings of attachment, relationship, nurturing, holding, touching." The male hormone is testosterone. Of it Wilbur says, "I don't mean to be crude, but it appears that testosterone basically has two, and only two, major drives: fuck it or kill it."[2]

To put it more gently, nature wants the young woman pregnant, so she is inclined to welcome lovers. He is more than happy to oblige. In fact he, following his nature, has the urge to plant his seed in as many women as possible. She must carry the resulting embryo for nine months, and nurse and care for the child for many years. Therefore she needs food and security which, because she is busy with her nursing, she cannot provide. His wandering ways also have limitations. He knows that, if his seed is to survive, the child must grow, so his instinct is to provide and protect.

Patriarchy appears

This sounds like an ideal set up. Perhaps the nearest we came to it actually working was way back in our age of innocence. Our biological roles were no doubt set before we had begun our consciousness journey. In a pre-conscious society, the woman, very naturally, has the place of honour, for she creates and nurtures life; hence the matriarchal, pre-Eve, period. We idealize that time, just as we do moments or periods in our own childhood. But with the coming of consciousness the innocent world is shattered, and patriarchy appears, with devastating results.

This happens because of an inherent imbalance of power.

The traditional female images are maid, mother, and crone (wise woman). We don't so often hear of the corresponding male images of youth, warrior, and sage. These deserve a whole discussion in themselves, but note that, in the mid years when our powers are at their height, we have on the female side mothers and on the male side warriors. This is an inherent imbalance of power, a setup for abuse.

The male, who is usually physically larger than the female and unencumbered by childbearing and rearing, can impose his will on women and children. He cannot as easily impose his will on other men, so he must fight, and war takes many forms. The competitive, aggressive, male spirit dominates business and government, as well as all our institutions, including religion, multinational corporations, and international politics.

Much has been accomplished, but. . .

The male style is not evil in itself. It creates and accomplishes, provides goods and security, all of which are necessary in our world. Much good has been achieved, but at a high price.

Patriarchy produced our scientific, technological age. We now have the technology to make the world one community. We can travel to practically any point on earth with relative ease. News flows quickly from wherever it happens. We can talk to most of the world by telephone. The Internet connects us to a world wide web of people and vast amounts of information. We can find the mystery and wisdom of every culture and religion at the bookstore or on the 'Net'. We live in a "global village."

Unfortunately, this powerful male thrust has also brought us to the brink of death. We have raped the earth and polluted the environment. Oppressive totalitarian regimes govern much of the world. Most of us are slaves to our economic systems. Many of us have become one-dimensional people, disconnected from our inner selves, our mythologies, and the divine. We are all victims, but women and children suffer most.

Patriarchy must end

Patriarchy must end. The process has begun, but we have far to go.

It will not be easy. Patriarchy permeates every institution: religion, government, education, law — everything. Yahweh, as a male sky god, has given patriarchy divine sanction. It is so deeply ingrained in our psychic and social structures that uprooting it, or transforming it, will take generations.

As males, we must awaken to our feminine, as well as our masculine. We cannot do away with our testosterone impulse, but we can develop psychic and social structures to make positive use of our aggressive energies. Our protective impulses must be used to build a safe and just world for all, which means doing away with patriarchy.

As females, you are ahead of us men in dealing with this issue. The oppressed are more keenly aware of their situation than the oppressor. The world, including all our institutions, badly need your healing and wholing nourishment. Both women and men must now offer their differing energies toward creating a world of justice and love where all are honoured and the gifts of each valued. We yearn for the day of true partnership to fully arrive.

Reflection questions

1. What do you think of patriarchy as a hard school of learning?
2. How are various roles you play in life (partner, parent, worker, church member) influenced by patriarchy?
3. What steps do you need to take to push forward toward equality of the sexes?

Your thoughts

21
A spunky woman
(Esther 1)

Queen Vashti is one of my favourite biblical people. Although on stage for only a few verses, she packs quite a wallop. In the book of Esther, a finely crafted tale on the supposed origins of the festival of Purim, she is the original queen.

The scene is "the court of the garden of the king's palace." (Esther 1:5b) Ahasuerus, king of the mighty empire of Media and Persia, throws a colossal party to show off his power and wealth. It lasts six months. He ends it with a great seven-day bash "for all the people present in the citadel of Susa, both great and small." (Esther 1:5a) The wine flows freely: "Drinking was by flagons, without restraint." (Esther 1:8)

As the festivities reach their zenith, the King has an idea. "He commanded [his attendants] to bring Queen Vashti before the king, wearing the royal crown [and presumably nothing more], in order to show the peoples and the officials her beauty; for she was fair to behold." (Esther 1:10-11)

Doing the unthinkable

Now comes the show stopper. "But Queen Vashti refused to come at the king's command." (Esther 1:12a) Refusing the command of the king was unthinkable. It could not happen. But it did. Vashti refused to compromise her dignity.

As she well knew, such action would have consequences. "At this the king was enraged, and his anger burned within him." (Esther 1:12b) His advisors, always attuned to political implications, quickly tell the king, "Not only has Queen Vashti done wrong to the king, but also to all the officials and all the peoples who are in all the provinces . . . . For this deed of the Queen will be made known to all women, causing them to look with contempt on their husbands . . . . This very day the noble ladies of Persia and Media who have heard of the queen's behaviour will rebel against the king's officials, and there will be no end of contempt and wrath!"

(Esther 1:16-18)

So Vashti is banished, and the king sends a proclamation throughout the kingdom to make sure that everyone will know. Now, "all women will give honour to their husbands, high and low alike . . . . [and] every man should be master in his own house." (Esther 1:20-22)

We may laugh, but they didn't. It was not intended to be funny.

A picture of patriarchy

The picture of patriarchy presented here seems to have not much changed until recent times.

My dictionary says that patriarchy is "a form of social organization in which the father is the supreme authority in the family, clan, or tribe," and that is the accepted social contract within this story. Male dominance was assumed and institutionalized. Any notion that a woman would have the right, or the courage, to say "no" to a male demand, no matter how outrageous, would not be tolerated. Vashti's disobedience did not bring patriarchy itself into question. She, not patriarchy, had to be dealt with.

The king banished Vashti. Amazingly, he did not summarily execute her.

But Vashti's act exposed the vulnerability of patriarchy. Allow an act of disobedience and the whole structure might come tumbling down. Action must be taken quickly and decisively, or women would get the wrong idea! They might catch on that males are not inherently superior.

This story illustrates that patriarchy will do whatever it must to maintain itself. We can expect that the more threatened patriarchy feels the more ferocious the response. We are not yet out of the woods.

Patriarchy in Bible and church

Confession is good for the soul, they say. We can start by facing up to the pervasive presence of patriarchy in both Bible and church. We must not try to explain it away. We must accept it as the social fabric within which the biblical story unfolds and which quickly engulfed the church.

With the emergence of feminism, much effort has been given to bringing to our attention the vital role of the women of the Bible, the feminine metaphors for God, seeing Wisdom as the feminine aspect of God, and the general presence of the feminine. We appreciate and applaud these developments. They help loosen the grip of patriarchy. They cannot, however, erase the fact that Yahweh was mainly understood as a male sky God, as more father than mother — and as a father who often had an attitude problem: petulant, judgmental, and angry.

Nor does the church escape

Jesus seems untarnished by the brush of patriarchy. But even he, according to the gospel accounts, had to succumb to the convention of male dominance by having twelve male disciples. Of course, the notion of twelve male disciples may be overplayed by the gospels. The writers, themselves the product of patriarchy, would naturally focus on the male disciples and relegate female disciples to the background. But even the gospel writers cannot hide the fact that there were women who travelled with Jesus, and, presumably, they were as much disciples as the men.

The shining light of equality that appeared in Jesus was quickly forced underground. Movements frequently turn into that which they originally opposed. The church instituted a hierarchical structure that was, and with some exceptions still is, diametrically opposite to the message it proclaimed. (I like to think that conciliar churches, like the United Church of Canada, have taken a different tone.) Fortunately, the message has been stronger than the structure. Even now, though, the Church is often the reluctant follower of society in recognizing women.

The church has much to answer for. It has upheld the patriarchy as divinely ordained, which has precipitated everything from the burning of witches to the subtle, and not so subtle, sidelining of women that continues to this day.

The age of patriarchy is over

I can talk about this only because of the many, mostly women, who have embodied and given voice to the feminine. It is through all those who refuse, like Vashti, to be intimidated by the forces of darkness that the light of truth shines. The Spirit will not be squelched.

The age of patriarchy is over, even if it takes generations to disappear.

Vashti, you are vindicated.

Reflection questions

1. I love the Vashti story. Don't you?
2. How has the Vashti picture of Patriarchy changed?
3. How has your image of the church been influenced by the church's patriarchal history?

Your thoughts

22
Wisdom
(Proverbs 1-9)

Naming God as Wisdom is an embarrassment in a patriarchal world. Wisdom, in Greek, is Sophia. Sophia is feminine and earthy, which does not fit easily into a male dominated religion.

Wisdom takes the attention away from the dominant, ruling, angry, sentimental, sky God and plants our feet in the nitty-gritty of life upon the earth. We find Wisdom in the thoroughfares of life. "Wisdom cries out in the street; in the squares she raises her voice. At the busiest corner she cries out; at the entrance of the city gates she speaks." (Proverbs 1:20-21) She cannot be relegated to the temple, where she could be kept safely contained. Wisdom is found in the midst of life.

The earthiness of Wisdom appealed to the Hebrews, for they were a gutsy, lusty people. The ascetic, body-denying approach did not emerge until New Testament times, with Paul and John and all those influenced by the Greek world. Oh, the Nazarites did deny themselves wine, and there were strict laws governing sexual relations and everything else, but basically the Hebrews believed in the body.

A problem for Yahweh

Yet celebrating and honouring the body, the feminine, the sexual, was a problem for the Hebrews. The sacred prostitution of the local religion took the focus away from following the will of the sky god. Yahweh, through prophets and priests, vigorously, even viciously, opposed any local religion that focused on nature, the earth, fertility, and the feminine. These views sound very narrow minded and exclusive, and they were. I believe, however, that they fulfilled a purpose in the development of human consciousness, but they left little room for the feminine.

The place of the feminine and the earthy, however, could not be totally denied. The relentless tirades against the Baals and the Asherah (local nature deities) indicates that their worship flourished. To be so popular and persistent they had to be meeting some deep need within the psyche of the Hebrew people.

What the religious purists tried to push out the front door came in the back door through the Wisdom literature. In Proverbs we have the amazing picture of Wisdom personified as the companion of God. This is the only such glimpse in the canonical (official) Bible, but what a potent, delightful passage.

"Ages ago I [Wisdom] was set up,
    at the first, before the beginning of the earth.
....
Before the mountains had been shaped,
before the hills, I was brought forth —
when [God] had not yet made earth and fields
or the world's first bits of soil.
When he established the heavens, I was there,
when he drew a circle on the face of the deep,
....
when he marked out the foundations of the earth,
then I was beside him, like a master worker;
and I was daily his delight,
rejoicing before him always,
rejoicing in his inhabited world
and delighting in the human race."
(Proverbs 8:23-31)

Not all commentators agree that Wisdom is here given divine status. I think, however, that we do have echoes of feminine divinities from surrounding religions and an acknowledgement that feminine Wisdom belongs within the Hebrew image of Yahweh.

Wisdom connecting heaven and earth

Accepting Wisdom as divine certainly helps to bring heaven and earth together. Wisdom is of the earth. She does not come as divine revelation from some "other" place. She is very down-to-earth and practical. She wants to help you get on as best you can in life. She finds truth by reflecting on the everyday experience of people, yet is the companion of God. In this way she imbues ordinary experience with divinity.

Wisdom literature in the Bible covers a wide range of human experience; sexuality (Song of Songs), spirituality (Psalms), suffering (Job), and mortality (Ecclesiastes), as well as the Wisdom found in the everyday experience of living (Proverbs).

Wisdom arises from and comments on these constant realities of life. Through the slow, patient drawing of conclusions from generations of experience, Wisdom grows. Wisdom is the original reflection (learning) process that we speak of so much in adult education. Through reflection Wisdom brings intelligence to bear on human experience.

The purpose of Wisdom's reflecting is to bring people to awareness. To act wisely means acting with awareness. You know what you are doing and why you are doing it. Wisdom, in that sense, represents the consciousness of creation.

Eros needs wisdom

To take it a step farther, Wisdom represents the feminine side of Yahweh. As the companion of Eros, she is the intelligence, the forming principle, behind the creation. She is God's operational arm. To get things going, God has to tap into Wisdom; she says, "I was set up, at the first, before the beginning of the earth."

The pure energy of Eros needs Wisdom to figure out how to create a satisfying partner. She, we can surmise, could see to it that creation emerged as a nourisher of consciousness. If Eros is the energy of creation, Wisdom is the planner, the architect, the one who sees that the creative energy produces results.

We need Wisdom

Wisdom still "cries to us from the street," still urges us to live with awareness. She delights both in God and "in the human race." She links us to our Source. She is the feminine within each one of us that keeps us grounded in the realities of life. She is the urge within us to unite spirit and body. Through her, we can become whole.

Sirach   a book that made it into the Roman Catholic Bible, but not the Protestant one — says:

"Search out and seek, and she will
become known to you;

and when you get hold of her,
do not let her go.
For at last you will find the rest she gives,
and she will be changed into
joy for you."
Sirrach 6:27-28)

Reflection questions

1. My partner, Emily, says that Sophia (the Greek word for Wisdom) sustained her through hard times. Is Sophia a "live" image for you?
2. How have you experienced Sophia?
3. In what ways can Sophia help in healing our relationship with the earth?

Your thoughts

23
The Word of God
(Isaiah 55; John 1:1-18)

Okay. So I got a bit carried away with the idea of God as Eros. Don't get me wrong. I'm not taking back anything I said. If I have to use only one word to describe the great Mystery, it is Eros.

But one word, of course, is not enough. No one word adequately encompasses the Ultimate Mystery. In recent years, we have become much more aware of the many words, images, metaphors — especially feminine ones — used in the Bible to describe God. The more images, the better we can grasp the expanse and depth of the mystery. A few words, however, have a special place. We can call them biblical archetypes of divinity. I am thinking of love, word, and wisdom; or, in their Greek form: Eros, Logos and Sophia.

Having already looked at Wisdom (Sophia), I want now to look at Word (Logos). But note that Sophia and Logos are in many ways interchangeable concepts, even though Sophia is presented as feminine and Logos as masculine.

We find Word as a name for God in the opening words of John's gospel. "In the beginning was the Word, and the Word was with God, and the word was God." (John 1:1)

Words and human nature

Since we can understand something of the nature of God by probing the depths of our own nature, we can ask what "word" says about us. We use words all the time but rarely think about their place in forming us.

"Word" has to do with communication, and communication is of the essence of the universe. Everything communicates with everything else at some level. Atoms communicate with other atoms. Animals have a quite sophisticated language. Humans believe, perhaps arrogantly, that we have developed language to a still higher level.

We use words in ordinary ways.

Words identify things. When I say tree, you conjure up an image of a tree. Your image may differ from mine, but we both recognize a tree. (Of course, understanding one another assumes we have a common language; diversity of language is another problem.)

Words also describe what objects do and how they relate. The tree grows. Again, we share an image of the tree getting bigger.

Thus we have nouns and verbs, things and how they relate. If we go into all the parts of speech, this discussion could get very complicated. But we need words to make us human. Our highly developed skill with language is a symbol of our being human.

Bridging our separateness

In one sense, we have been forced to develop language because of our aloneness. Stepping into consciousness separates and isolates us. Language represents our effort to bridge the gap of separation. My isolated self wants to commune with your isolated self, and using words (and other art forms) is a way of doing that. In fact, I have no way of knowing my inner world without having it reflected back to me by sharing thoughts with other people, and words are the vehicle.

Helen Keller, who had neither sight nor hearing, illustrates the importance of language. Because of her impairments, making the connection between words and things proved nearly impossible. She was left with a desperate loneliness. Finally one day, as her teacher pumped water over her hands and then tapped the code, she made the breakthrough. A certain sequence of taps meant water. The things she touched and experienced could be translated into taps. She had discovered words. The whole world opened up to her. Now she had a way of sorting out the world around her and communicating. We so easily take language for granted!

Words are not the ultimate communication. We dream that our words will lead to a time when we do not need words, when the separation has been overcome. In our intimate moments, we commune without words, whether it be with nature, God, or another person. Jeremiah had a vision of a time when "no longer shall they teach one another, or say to each other, 'Know the Lord,' for they shall all know me, from the least of them to the greatest." (Jeremiah 31:34) Preaching and teaching, even these words of mine, would be unnecessary!

We need words to bridge our brokenness and incompleteness. But the final word is the silence of communion and oneness.

The nature of God

What does our exploration of "word" tell us about the nature of God?

Word is a metaphor for the creative activity of God. "God said, 'Let there be light'; and there was light" (Genesis 1:3) God speaks, and it happens. We use words to create from what has already been created. God uses words to create out of nothing.

Eros must create. Just as we need the universe and other people to experience who we are, so also does God. Eros cannot be realized without Logos, without a relationship with creation. We cannot love without something or someone to love. To continue the words of John's gospel, "All things came into being through him [the Word], and without him not one thing came into being." (John 1:3)

The Word continues to create. "My word . . . that goes out from my mouth . . . shall not return to me empty, but it shall accomplish that which I purpose, and succeed in the thing for which I sent it." (Isaiah 55:11) The Word is out there continually and relentlessly at work, all the time seeking to bring life, and the universe, to wholeness. The Bible is the story of the activity of the Word.

A major step toward that end was taken when "the Word became flesh and lived among us." (John 1:14) Jesus the Christ then becomes the vehicle through which "all of us come . . . to maturity, to the measure of the full stature of Christ." (Ephesians 4:13)

The Word of God, then, is the yearning Eros creating a mature humanity. God, too, yearns for a time of the ultimate communion of no words. In the final vision of the New Jerusalem in Revelation, the writer says, "I saw no temple in the city." (Revelation 21:22) There is no need for a place of words or of ritual. Heaven has come to earth. The separation between God and humanity has been healed.

The challenge to us

God's Word appears in each of us as the nagging, gnawing, coaxing, creative energy that wants us to be our true and full selves.

The same can be said of Sophia.

For me, this means that Logos and Sophia, the creating, wholing activity of Eros, is always and everywhere at work. The promise is that they "will succeed in the thing for which I [Eros] sent (them)." (Isaiah 55:11b) The challenge to us as hearers and bearers of Word and Wisdom is to be true partners in the process.

Reflection questions

1. Do you experience Word as active in your life?
2. Sophia and Logos have a different flavour, Sophia bringing warm encouragement and Logos being a demanding voice. Do you feel both these forces at work in you, or one more than the other?
3. In what ways have you resisted heeding the Word?

Your thoughts

24
Incarnation
(The Central Concept Of The Christian Bible)

We seldom use the word incarnation in general conversation. In my youth, I heard an occasional reference to so and so, who had done something especially terrible, being "the devil incarnate." We do hear it at Christmas when there is talk about God becoming incarnate in Jesus.

When we connect Jesus and incarnation, we are into a big subject. God becoming human is the whole story of the Christian Bible. This means that the whole meaning and thrust of life is toward incarnation. God becomes incarnate in humanity, and humanity incarnates God.

To make real in this world

My dictionary defines incarnate as "to embody in flesh; invest with a body, esp. a human form." In other words, incarnation is the process of translating something from imagination, thought, myth or somewhere into here-and-now existence in this world.

Everything from an idea to a quality to a divinity can be incarnated. Last summer, Emily and I built, or incarnated, a boat ramp. We had the wish, the idea. We wanted a ramp. We planned. What did we need it to do? How long and wide should it be? What materials did we need? Then we had to buy them, bring them home, put them together, and put the ramp in place. I skip over the lengthy discussions, which could easily degenerate into disagreements, but finally there it was. A want, an idea, had become a reality.

The ramp was relatively easy. Other things, like these Think Pieces, require more of me.

We are always in the process of incarnating something into reality. The carpenter builds a house. The artist creates a painting. The teacher facilitates learning. The thinker develops ideas. Parents bring forth a child. Incarnation is the process of life.

The biggest challenge for us is incarnating our own lives.

Every human being, and no doubt every aspect of the universe, wants to have a good life, whatever that may mean. We want to actually live out in the flesh and blood of history the truth and purpose of our lives.

The task of life

"Who am I?" is the most persistent of questions. We live with ourselves all our lives and still don't know ourselves completely. Some say we are like an onion. We take off one layer only to discover another, and then another. Perhaps we are an infinite onion with no end to the layers! Uncovering and living our true lives takes a lifetime.

Within each one of us is a larger self struggling to be born. It seems we always want to have more, do more, be more.

Often we assume that this self is hidden somewhere deep within. We yearn for the time and opportunity for meditative reflection that will enable us to find and own that hidden self. We are right. We do need quiet time.

Yet the raw material for our reflection comes from the rough-and-tumble of life. Situations and experiences, both positive and negative, help us discover parts of ourselves. A confrontation with the boss, an awakening to injustice, a friend, a relationship, a new job, a discovered interest, a community crisis, a family tragedy, the necessity of making a living — all that life brings provides the rich soil for self discovery.

However it happens, we need to attend to our unique response. What is our inner voice or self saying? Who am I in this situation? What do I feel? What do I think? What do I need to do? Have I been true to myself? What have I learned about myself and life?

For me, life has been a process of going out into the world and doing things and then, battered and bruised, returning to my inner self and taking a step on my inner journey, then going out into the world again, and so on. Both in and out seem necessary to the slow process of becoming what I am able to be, of incarnating the fullness of my self.

I have seen the same thing in people who come to Tatamagouche Centre, where I worked for eight years. They have one, or both, of two main agendas: to learn skills for helping the world (community, family, church, country, environment, developing world, etc.); or to uncover and be their real selves in the various aspects of their lives. They want to incarnate a society that reflects the full humanness of life and in the process to incarnate their own lives. So we can begin either with ourselves or with the world, but both are necessary.

Hard-won and hard-held

Incarnation is a rough road. We are always under pressure to meet the expectations of others (peers, parents, partners, church, government, boss). Being true to one's self and living with justice, compassion, and integrity in a world that seems to honour none of these things is a tall order.

Living in the sheltered cocoon of developed countries makes it nearly impossible for us to glimpse the cruelty, injustice, torture, and intimidation that most of the world must endure. We also build protective cocoons within ourselves to keep the ferocity of our inner battles at bay. Struggling to be a free people or free selves can come at a high price. Any small victory is hard-won and hard-held.

We all take stabs at it. Few have managed it in any complete way. The easy thing is to fit in, to keep your head down, and not make waves. But those who have risen above the crowd are the shining lights that draw humanity on. We have Jesus, Buddha, Socrates, Gandhi, Martin Luther King Jr., Nelson Mandela and a long list; a "great . . . cloud of witnesses." (Hebrews 12:1) We know that some of them certainly were not perfect, but they did bring their unique selves and gifts to the world.

We all have our contribution to make. Incarnation is the process that makes it happen. But if we expect life to be easy, Christianity gives us a very bad model. Look what Jesus had to go through to incarnate who he was in the world.

We are not expected to be Jesus, but we are expected to be ourselves. The question put to your life and mine is not "Why are you not Jesus?" but "Why are you not you?"

Reflection questions

1. What have you "incarnated" in the world?
2. How is the challenge of incarnating your potential going?
3. How do you deal with the gap between who you are and who
   you could be?

Your thoughts

25
The urge to incarnate
(The Need Of Eros To Become Human)

Why is history so important? What makes the ordinary day-by-day stuff of our lives so full of meaning, at least most of the time? Why do we go through such agony trying to live out the truth of our lives?

The simple answer is that life happens in everyday living or it does not happen at all. At an even more basic level, if we did not believe that our lives are important, we would not have the drive to survive, and we wouldn't be here.

Even deeper questions arise. Why does the universe want us here? Is there any cosmic significance to our lives?

I have intimated that I believe there is more than our own lives at stake. Certainly in the interpretation of the Christian myth presented here, and awakening in our contemporary awareness, is the notion that without us the universe cannot become whole or complete.

Put another way, Yahweh needs humanity in order to become fully God. If this is true, our lives have cosmic value, and human history takes on cosmic significance.

History is important to God

Being created in the image of divinity means that the deeply important aspects of our lives must also be valued at the Mythic and Ultimate levels. The living of history must have ultimate value for Eros as well as for us.

It seems that Eros/Yahweh needs the nitty-grittiness of history in order to know and enjoy the fullness of being God. Eros cannot be Eros without incarnation, without entering into the solid stuff of history. Incarnation, then, is not only the purpose and goal of our lives, but also the telos (ultimate goal) of God.

Getting there is not easy, even for God.

We know the difficulty of incarnating our own lives, but it is our nature to try. It must be the same with God.

We incarnate ourselves, become visible, in what we say, do and create. In every aspect of our lives, we are creating. We create a meal, a clean house, a song (one of Emily's gifts that remains a mystery to me), an institution, a work of art, a marriage (hetero-sexual, homosexual, or whatever), a community, or whatever. Through our doing, our creating, we gradually incarnate ourselves and the community of humanity.

Rarely, though, does a single word, action or creation fully express who we are. Fortunate, and fulfilled, is the person who can put out something that reflects their total being. For me, creat-ing the boat ramp was an interesting but almost incidental crea-tion. Writing these Think Pieces requires a much bigger part of me. They are a way of incarnating my purpose in the world.

Like God, we are both in and not in what we create. What I say, do, create, must have something of me in it. Woe to me when it does not. One of the insights of my life came when I realized I was so busy doing so many things that there was little or nothing of me in anything I did. At times, at least, we need to go deep into ourselves to come up with what authentically represents us.

Human history is the story of God's struggle to incarnate what truly represents God in the world.

In the Christian myth, the human story gets under way with Eve eating the fruit, stepping into consciousness. It ends with the New Jerusalem descending from God out of heaven — a final incarnation where humanity becomes a true vessel for containing God. This venture into consciousness is the biblical story, and, I believe, the human story.

Yahweh, the becoming God

What is true for humanity also applies to Yahweh, the central God-image of the Old Testament. Yahweh, too, must grow to maturity. We first meet a petulant, judgmental, immature Yahweh. But we also meet a Yahweh who yearns for humanity, whose love is con-stant and compelling.

Listen to Yahweh yearning for Israel: (Hosea 11:1-8)
When Israel was a child, I loved him,
and out of Egypt I called my son.

The more I called them, the more they went from me . . . .
Yet it was I who taught Ephraim to walk,
I took them up in my arms;
but they did not know that I healed them.
I led them with cords of human kindness,
with bands of love.
I was to them like those who lift infants to their cheeks.
I bent down to them and fed them . . .
How can I give you up, Ephraim? . . .

....

My heart recoils within me;
my compassion grows warm and tender."
Yahweh also makes mature demands that draw us to maturity:
"What does the Lord require of you but to do justice, and to love
kindness, and to walk humbly with your God." (Micah 6:8) Loving kindness, the Hebrew word *chesed*, is a constant Old Testament description of the yearning Yahweh.

Yahweh's partners — the various selves of Yahweh — Wisdom (Sophia), Word (Logos), and finally Christ, help the process.

The Christ archetype, lived out in the person of Jesus, is the
ultimate witness to the need of Eros/Yahweh to incarnate in history, and the central message of the Christian Bible. The incarnating of the Christ energy, and Jesus as the Christ, is vitally important to the human and divine journey. It will occupy my attention
for most of the remainder of this book.

Reflection questions

1. Does the idea of Eros yearning for humanity to become whole ring true for you?
2. What facets of history interest you, and what does that say about your personal contribution to history?
3. What role are you playing in the divine-human drama?

Your thoughts

26
The dark side of incarnation
(Matthew 2:16-18)

"When Herod saw that he had been tricked by the wise men, he was infuriated, and he sent and killed all the children in and around Bethlehem who were two years old or under." (Matthew 2:16) This story from the Christmas mythology of Matthew's gospel comes as a jarring note amid joyous celebrations. Our Christmas pageants do not include it.

The slaughter of the innocents

This story, aptly named "The slaughter of the innocents," brings us down from our Christmas high with a dull thud. The evil of the world confronts us. The suffering and slaughter of the innocent children symbolize the story of humanity. Reflected in this incident is all the innocent suffering of the world. Injustice, oppression, famine, and war leave a devastation that I shrink from imagining, although television brings its nightly litany.

Nor is it all happening in far-off countries from which we can feel detached. Look at our own society. When our security as middle and upper-income people is threatened, we make war on the poor, children, women, immigrants, minorities, single mothers, homosexuals, the aged. . . This list goes on. And on.

We can easily see physical atrocities. Psychic damage is harder to document. How can a people who have suffered generations of oppression find the inner strength to survive, let alone struggle for justice? The Exodus was such a situation, and one that speaks to many oppressed peoples.

We all suffer the ravages of growing up and living in a screwed-up world. As a psychiatrist friend told me, "The line outside my door just keeps getting longer and longer." I remember my eldest daughter saying to me, "Dad, you never taught us what a vicious world it is out there."

In this vicious world, we must pay serious attention to the reality of evil.

I have taken care to make clear that creation is good. "God saw everything that [God] had made, and indeed, it was very good." (Genesis 1:31) I have also affirmed my belief that Eros is everywhere and always at work; the word "that goes out from my mouth . . . shall not return to me empty." (Isaiah 55:11) In spite of this, we cannot escape the dark side of life.

Consciousness and evil

With all this goodness, why is there evil?

Enter consciousness, whose work is to bring the shadow, unknown, sometimes evil side of our beings to full awareness.

I have laid the groundwork in looking at Eve, at patriarchy, and in other places, but now it's time for a deeper plunge. I never want to lose sight of Eve as a heroine. She symbolizes our entering upon the journey to maturity. Unfortunately, opening the door of consciousness also thrusts us into the murky world of evil.

Human consciousness was something new upon the earth. Creation now took on a new quality. Independence and freedom came into play. Eve made her own decision, against the advice of God. Disobedience is the first mark of independent awareness. We see it when a child first learns the power of "no."

Yahweh finally accepted that humanity must be allowed conscious free will. Yahweh had moments of grave doubt (e.g., Noah and the flood) but ultimately did not take free will from us. We are, for good or ill, responsible for our own actions. We must live with the results of our decisions. Yahweh cannot, or will not, short-circuit the process. Yahweh will not rescue us from our short-sightedness and stupidity or, in any direct way, from the maliciousness and stupidity of others.

We are created with the capacity for consciousness, but the actual coming to awareness we must learn through our own experience. There is no other way.

There is much to learn, and the road is long. Jung spoke of us being little islands of consciousness in the large sea of the unconscious. This vast unknown Jung called the shadow, and it lurks within us with both demonic and saving power.

Evil and the relentlessly yearning Eros

Be reminded that Eros is everywhere and always at work. Eros yearns for incarnation, wants to be fully embodied. Even our hidden energy, our shadow side, wants to incarnate into consciousness. As I write this, the radio is playing "The World is Always Turning Toward the Morning." Eros is eternally optimistic.

The mixture of hope and fear in us will always try to construct a world to fit our own little picture, which Jung calls the ego. Vast areas of the self remain unknown, but the energy of this shadow side never ceases working. When, in our ignorance, we act against the interest of our self or of the grand Self, that energy will turn on us and become demonic. In our ignorance, we let loose the energies that will seek to destroy our small, incomplete, and imperfect world. Evil is the energy of the shadow that turns against us.

On the positive side, our small, imperfect selves must die before a more complete self can be born. Evil, in the long run, brings about good, but not without a price.

A hard way to learn

What a painful way to learn! Until we know the fullness of who we are, we will always make bad decisions. Our view is always too narrow, our vision too self-centred and incomplete. The history of the world stands as witness to the death and carnage we bring upon ourselves and one another.

Eros is stuck with us. The universe may well contain other centres of consciousness, but we are at least one cosmic experiment through whom Eros seeks to create a loving partner. Eros/Yahweh must find us a painful and frustrating lot. The relentless longing to incarnate comes up against our "hardness of heart," our slowness to learn. In the meantime, our resistance to becoming whole wreaks havoc among us.

The Bible gives us glimpses of the yearning, and often frustrated, Yahweh seeking to become incarnate. At the same time, it is the story of our seeking to grow to our fullness. Human history is the arena of both Yahweh's yearning and our learning.

We are challenged to become a suitable and delightful partner for the yearning Eros/Yahweh before our foolishness destroys us.

Reflection questions

1. What are some of the evils of the world that especially trouble you?
2. How do we as individuals and as a society contribute to injustice and devastation, to people and to the earth?
3. How do you deal with your own dark side?

Your thoughts

Notes

1. Aristophanes. *Lysistrata.*
2. Ken Wilber. *A Brief History of Everything.* (Boston, Massachusetts: Shambala Publications, Inc., 1975), p. 4.

Jesus

Holy of Holies

Holy of Holies, great energy.
yearning of Eros created me.
Holy of Holies, deep mystery,
Eros, I name you Divinity.

Come let us all be lovers in time,
Come, let us all be lovers on earth
for when the soul in me
knows the soul in you
it is then (it is then) that Eros gives birth,

I behold a baby's smile, and that is grace.
In my lover's arms I find a sacred place.
Holy of Holies, great energy,
Eros, I name you divinity.

Spirit of the Universe, You call to me,
Luring me and all that lives to life that's free.
Holy One, Creator of galaxies,
Eros, I name you Divinity.

Emily Kierstead

27
Jesus' birth
(Matthew 1-2; Luke 1-2)

The stories surrounding Jesus' birth are not really about Jesus' birth. Any actual history they contain (beyond his mother's name) is now impossible to sort out from the mythology.

The familiar Christmas stories emerged in the church to help explain the extraordinary quality of the person Jesus. Early Christians, like every generation since, were trying to find ways of expressing the wonder and power of the person they met in Jesus. They chose a way common to their time and developed a virgin birth mythology, and pageantry to go with it.

The mythic stories

There were probably no shepherds or wise men. Jesus was no doubt conceived in the usual way. There was no donkey ride to Bethlehem (later mythology added the donkey) or flight into Egypt, and, mercifully, no slaughter of the innocents.

Yet we can honour the mythology and enjoy the Christmas pageantry as a legitimate expression of the Christian faith. (What modern marketing has done with Christmas is another issue.)

Matthew and Luke are our sources. They alone of the New Testament writers give us birth legends. Matthew's story gives us the wise men, and Luke contributes the shepherds. Their accounts differ, and only in Christmas pageantry can they fit together.

There are similarities. In both accounts, Mary is Jesus' mother and Joseph her about-to-be husband. The birth takes place in Bethlehem (near Jerusalem), but Jesus grows up in Nazareth (a town in Galilee).

Both agree that Jesus was born of a virgin. Matthew says, "Now the birth of Jesus the Messiah took place in this way. When his mother Mary had been engaged to Joseph, but before they lived together, she was found to be with child from the Holy Spirit." (Matthew 1:18)

Luke, in a longer, more eloquent account, tells of the angel

Gabriel visiting Mary and saying, "'And now, you will conceive
in your womb and bear a son, and you will name him Jesus' . . . .
Mary said to the angel, 'How can this be since I am a virgin?' The
angel said to her, 'The Holy Spirit will come upon you, and the
power of the Most High shall overshadow you'."(Luke 1:31, 34-
35) Although "virgin," in Hebrew, means young woman, Matthew
and Luke are clearly saying that Jesus was conceived without sexual
intercourse.

Virgin birth

The virgin birth stories represent one phase in the evolving awareness of who Jesus was. Mark, the earliest gospel written about 70
CE, does not mention Jesus' birth at all. (Nor do Paul's letters,
which pre-date all the gospels.) Telling of Jesus' ministry was most
important at that point. Ten years later, when Matthew and Luke's
gospels were written, speculation about Jesus' origins had come
to the fore. The virgin birth mythologies were the response. Toward the end of the century, when John's gospel was written, Jesus' coming moves into a cosmic context: "The Word [the Logos
of God] became flesh and lived among us." (John 1:14)

The vivid and eloquent Christmas stories have completely captured our imaginations. Anyone with the vaguest connection with
the church cannot imagine Christmas without creche scenes and
pageantry. Even shopping malls give us glimpses of the original
mythology. We enjoy being swept along by the feelings of love
and good will. And so we should, for a very special expression of
love did come into the world in Jesus.

The downside of a doctrine

These stories have a downside, of which we need to be aware.
Read Bishop John Shelby Spong's *Born of a Woman*, if you want
an extended discussion.

Mary as virgin and mother has become a symbol or archetype
of the ideal woman. As someone has said, the Bible presents the
images of virgin and mother but does not provide much help in
getting from one to the other. The virgin route to motherhood is
becoming more possible (artificial insemination, *in vitro* fertiliza-

tion, etc.) but it's still not the usual option for most women!

These submissive images suited the purposes of the patriarchy. Being fearful of the power of the feminine, they favoured seeing women in "safe" roles. "Virgin" does not project the sexual potency of the feminine. And "mother" focuses on the nurturing role, keeping the woman safely busy and out of men's hair.

The patriarchy needed another feminine model upon whom to project their sexual fantasies, so they painted Mary Magdalene as a prostitute. (Actually, she seems to have been the foremost of the female disciples who followed Jesus.)

Virgin, mother, and prostitute are all roles controllable by men. Limiting womanhood in this way meant that men did not have to deal with the full personhood of sexually powerful women. These images supported the patriarchal denial of the feminine and the denigration of women.

Another downside of the virgin birth mythology is that it compromises Jesus' humanity. If Jesus was virgin born and Mary was "with child from the Holy Spirit," then he was more than human and, therefore, essentially different from the rest of us. If virgin born, he loses all credibility as a model of what it means to be human, or as a leader on the journey to full humanity.

Divine involvement

Matthew and Luke both assert that the divine was involved in Jesus' birth. I agree, but then I believe that the divine is involved with the birth of each of us. I believe that what happened with Jesus was not categorically different from the birth process we all go through. Our true being emerges out of some kind of cosmic process that says, "You have a special and unique place." Jesus' uniqueness came from his special role as the incarnate Messiah and how completely he fulfilled it.

We need not believe in the virgin birth to be Christian. We need only to affirm that the divine was involved with Jesus' birth and that in Jesus a very special person lived upon this earth.

So enjoy the rich pageantry of Christmas. Reality comes to us through much more than the literal and the rational. Celebrate the coming of an embodiment of love.

Reflection questions

1. Are there aspects of our Christmas celebrations that trouble you?
2. What aspects of our Christmas celebrations do you affirm and enjoy?
3. What truth do you discover in the mythic stories?

Your thoughts

28
Jesus' baptism
(Matthew 3; Mark 1:2-11; Luke 3; John 1:19-34)

We have an elemental relationship with water. Our bodies are mostly water. Our genes remember that, in our evolution, we spent a long time in water. I love to look at water. Our home is on a lake, and every day the water has a different look. Perhaps it is my dour Scottish ancestry, but I love a misty, rainy day. Sun glistening on the wet leaves also brings refreshment to the soul. Ocean waves thundering onto the shore resonate to my very core.

We are born out of water. When the woman's water breaks, birth is imminent. I remember well my excitement and panic when my wife's gushing water sent us speeding to the hospital.

Baptism is the ritual of spiritual birth. Water is the symbolic element. Sprinkling, pouring, or immersing, the symbolic action.

In the baptism of a child, the parents wed themselves and their child to the church as a womb of spiritual birthing. The sprinkling or pouring of water on the child's head invites the Holy Spirit as the birthing energy.

Adult baptism is the public ritual of our spiritual call and commitment. Immersion is the powerful act. Going down into the water we drown to the old. Rising from the water we are born anew.

John the Baptizer
John the Baptizer was a strange one, even among the itinerant charismatic teachers who roamed the Palestine of Jesus' day. "Now John was clothed with camel's hair, with a leather belt around his waist, and he ate locusts and wild honey." (Mark 1:6) John was a wild-eyed desert dweller, "proclaiming a baptism of repentance for the forgiveness of sins." (Mark 1:4)

He may sound crazy, but he wasn't. Luke records the tradition that he came from a priestly family. Perhaps he had spent time with the Essenes, a recluse community who had withdrawn to the edge of the Dead Sea to maintain their purity while waiting for a Teacher of Righteousness.

Whatever his background, John was a holy man of the desert. The messiah fever of the time took hold of him and sent him out as "the voice of one crying out in the wilderness: 'Prepare the way of the Lord'." (Mark 1:3) The crowds came, "filled with expectation, . . . [wondering] whether he might be the Messiah." (Luke 3:15) John was very clear that he was not the Messiah: "The one who is more powerful than I is coming after me; I am not worthy to stoop down and untie the thong of his sandals. I have baptized you with water; but he will baptize you with the Holy Spirit." (Mark 1:7-8)

The crowds tagged John as "the baptizer" because baptizing was unusual. It was not a traditional Jewish rite. John borrowed it (perhaps from the Essenes) or developed it as an initiation ritual into his community of messianic expectation.

Jesus chooses baptism

So "in those days Jesus came from Nazareth of Galilee and was baptized by John in the Jordan." (Mark 1:9)

How long Jesus had been listening to John's preaching we do not know. In Mark's account, this is the first we hear of him. Mark gives us no clue to his birth or early life. We later discover that he was 30 years old, a traditional age for setting out on one's life work. Apparently, he was deeply attracted to John's vision, so much so that he joined the movement by being baptized.

We can only surmise Jesus' inner thoughts. We have the story of the young twelve-year-old Jesus visiting the Jerusalem temple (Luke 2:41-52). Even if not historical, it conveys his avid interest in learning all he could about his tradition. We know that Nazareth had a good synagogue where he would have received some formal education. He had the opportunity to become steeped in his tradition.

No doubt Jesus felt the messiah energy that swirled about. He must have felt a deep stirring and pondered what it might mean for him. We can assume that something more than a chance venture brought him to where John the Baptizer was doing his thing. The details of the inner journey that led Jesus to the edge of the Jordan that day we will never know.

His call

But we do know that as Jesus came up out of the water, something momentous happened. "He saw the heavens torn apart and the Spirit descending like a dove on him. And a voice came from heaven, 'You are my Son, the Beloved; with you I am well pleased'." (Mark 1:10-11) It was an awesome, mystic, revelatory moment. His life could never be the same again.

This was the moment of Jesus' call. The meaning of all that had gone on in him and around him suddenly broke into his consciousness. The yearning for a Messiah, so intense among the people, took form in him, and suddenly he knew himself as the chosen one.

As the beloved of God, he must now live out his role as the Messiah. He had to embody and live the divine Eros as a human person. Job had reached the point of self-possession where he could confront Yahweh in righteous indignation. Now Jesus had to "take on" Yahweh/God at a whole new level. His own self had to be big enough and strong enough to live among humanity as total love.

Our call

Not much wonder that "the Spirit immediately drove him out into the wilderness." (Mark 1:12) He needed time to allow the momentousness of his call to sink in. He also had to figure out how to go about living it.

His dramatic introduction to his destiny was beyond what happens to most of us. Our "calls" are usually not that clear or complete, but we do have our own baptismal moments. Intimations, dreams, perhaps mystical experiences that point us this way or that do come to us, and we need to pay attention. They can sharpen our awareness of the purpose of our lives.

Whatever our calling or destiny, we can give thanks that our piece of the puzzle is much smaller than the one given to Jesus! Yet, without each of us, the picture is incomplete. Even as Jesus did, we need to attend to and follow the call of life.

Reflection questions

1. If you have been baptized, what does it mean for you?
2. Have you ever felt called, baptized, into a particular task, role or destiny and how did you respond?
3. What baptism rituals could we develop to mark occasions when we feel called?

Your thoughts

29
Conquering temptation
(Matthew 4:1-11; Mark 1:12-13; Luke 4:1-13)

Someone has said, "The hardest thing about being Christian is trying to distinguish between temptation and opportunity." I'm not sure the problem is specifically Christian, for everyone encounters it, but Jesus certainly had to deal with it a number of times.

The challenge for Jesus, as for all of us, was to figure out how he could with integrity live out his calling. The momentous destiny which met him upped the ante. He dare not be wrong. What a tragedy if the Messiah blew it!

Fortunately for Jesus, his destiny became clear to him. Most of us only slowly uncover a sense of purpose, and sorting out temptation from opportunity amid the competing possibilities, needs, and responsibilities of life is an imperfect art. That issue now confronted Jesus.

After the heavens opened, the dove descended, and the voice spoke (all symbols of a profound inner experience of the call of God, or the Self), Jesus was driven into the wilderness. "He was in the wilderness forty days, tempted by Satan; and he was with the wild beasts; and the angels waited on him." (Mark 1:13) The wild beasts were no doubt mostly inner ones, as were the angels who cared for him. Jesus was in a classic, cosmic struggle to figure out the way he should go.

The temptation to do good

His first temptation, according to both Matthew and Luke, was to turn stones into bread. His own hunger no doubt triggered it. The thought must have come to him that if he had messiah powers he could use them to meet the immediate physical needs of the world. That must have seemed like a worthy goal that would save many lives and make many people happy. Later in his ministry, he would in fact feed a crowd of five thousand. But should this be the chief aim of his ministry?

He could feed the hungry, but was it an opportunity or a temptation? To answer that question, Jesus must have delved deeply into himself and into the reservoir of wisdom from his tradition that rang true for him. "One does not live by bread alone," (Luke 4:4) came as his answer.

Jean Houston's oft-repeated exhortation, "Don't waste your time doing good things, you only have time to do your best" (which I heard while attending her Mystery School), sums up the situation. Jesus followed that dictum. Feeding the hungry would be a good thing, but not his main focus as the Messiah.

The temptation of power

Satan blatantly tempted Jesus with political power (the second temptation in Luke, third in Matthew). "Then the devil led [Jesus] up and showed him in an instant all the kingdoms of the world. And the devil said to him, 'To you I will give their glory and all this authority . . . . If you, then, will worship me, it will all be yours'." (Luke 4:5-7)

Surely establishing the rule of love was a worthy purpose. Was political power the way to do it? The popular expectation that the Messiah would be a political leader must have added to the tension. Establishing political power would meet the popular demand. Could it do more? Was this an opportunity or a temptation?

Again, Jesus went deep. Hebrew history surely proved that political power did not work. Becoming a nation had ended in disaster. Their country was laid waste, and they had been exiled. In Jesus' time, centuries later, Rome ruled them. Jesus would be quite aware of these failures of political power.

The Arthurian legends of the quest for the Holy Grail come to mind. They ask, "Whom does the Grail serve?" Jesus asked, "Whom does the Messiah serve?" We all need to ask, "Ultimately, whom do we serve?" The answer must be that when we serve the larger purpose of life, we serve God. Jesus answered, "It is written, 'Worship the Lord your God, and serve only [God]'." (Luke 4:8)

Love is not served by external, coercive power. Jesus would have to find some other way to carry out his purpose.

Tempting God

Then comes the "show off" temptation. We are easily tempted "to think of yourself more [or less] highly than you ought to think" (Romans 12:3), and act accordingly. People often follow charismatic leaders with inflated egos.

The temptation was real. How did Jesus handle it? In his vision, "The devil took him to Jerusalem, and placed him on the pinnacle of the temple, saying to him, 'If you are the Son of God, throw yourself down from here'." (Luke 4:9) Such a stunt would attract the attention of large numbers of people by showing off his spectacular powers. Was it an opportunity or a temptation?

Even if Jesus could pull it off, what would he accomplish? Superficial heroism does not serve love. Nothing in this spectacle speaks to the transformation of the soul.

Again going to a deeper level, Jesus saw it as a tempting of God. "Do not put the Lord your God to the test." (Luke 4:12) Do not expect God to support our inflated opinion of ourselves, or magically get us out of a mess. Love does not work that way.

So ended this round of temptation. "When the devil had finished every test, he departed from him until an opportune time." (Luke 4:13) We know not when, where, or how temptation will return, but return it will.

Left with our humanity

In the meantime, Jesus was left knowing he had no extraordinary way to carry out his mission. All that he had was the strength and quality of his own humanity.

Jesus' inner strength, solidness, and awareness greatly impresses me. Job had been strong enough to confront Yahwch. Jesus took that inner development another giant step by having the self possession to face powerful temptations and set out on his mission with only his humanity.

It was no small feat for Jesus, and a challenge to us.

✧ ✧ ✧

Reflection questions

1. When have you been tempted to misuse or fail to use your strengths?
2. What is your greatest current temptation?
3. What are some of the ways we have collectively succumbed to temptation?

Your thoughts

30
Jesus the teacher
(The four gospels)

We have been inoculated. We are immune. We don't catch on to the radicalness of Jesus' teaching. Granted, we live in a very different world. We may not always understand the background and context, nor do we have the impact of his presence. Yet his words and actions ring down through time with an authenticity and power which confronts us with the pure essence of life and what it requires of us.

The Kingdom of God comes near

Jesus began his ministry with no great fanfare. When the opportunity came, he picked up the mantle of John the Baptizer and gave it his own twist. "Now after John was arrested, Jesus came to Galilee, proclaiming the good news of God, and saying, 'The time is fulfilled, and the kingdom of God has come near; repent, and believe in the good news'." (Mark 1:14-15)

Among a people oppressed by Roman rule, talk of another kingdom was good news. People would feel an inner thrill of possibility and travel great distances to hear him. Add to this his healing work, and we can understand why "the common people heard him gladly." (Mark 12:37 KJV)

Gradually, though, it became obvious that Jesus was talking about something other than political rule. The realm of God is where love rules, and that must be in the heart as well as in the social order. It involves the political, for it means the building of a just, loving, and compassionate society, but also includes the transformation of the soul.

The first clue that citizenship in this new realm would be demanding comes in the word "repent." To repent means to change direction. Instead of living one way, we must live another. Social systems, belief systems, and lifestyles must change.

Love is the message

Love is the guiding principle and the whole of Jesus' message.

There is nothing gushy or sentimental about Jesus' talk of love. He taught and lived a tough love. Hear some of his words: "Love your enemies and pray for those who persecute you." (Matthew 5:44) "Do not resist an evildoer. But if anyone strikes you on the right cheek, turn the other also; and if anyone wants to sue you and take your coat, give your cloak as well; and if anyone forces you to go one mile, go also the second mile. Give to everyone who begs from you, and do not refuse anyone who wants to borrow from you." (Matthew 5:39-42)

Would you, could you, do these things? I find most of that teaching totally impractical. As I quote that passage, I mentally select the more reasonable parts. Going the second mile sounds possible, but giving to everyone who begs or wants to borrow seems a bit much, and in much of the world totally impossible. And what can you make of not resisting an evildoer?

Jesus does not focus on the easy or practical but on what pure love would want to do. He imposes no limits. Peter asked Jesus, "'How often should I forgive? As many as seven times?' Jesus said to him, 'Not seven times, but . . . *seventy times seven*'" (alternate translation in NRSV footnote). (Matthew 18:21-22) Jesus was not talking about 490 times, but infinity.

Jesus usually taught by parable; by telling stories that illustrate how love operates. Luke records some of the best loved: "The Good Samaritan" (Luke 10:29-37), to the Hebrews an oxymoron, (for "Samaritan" you can substitute whatever minority on whom you project your inadequacies); "The Prodigal Son" (Luke 15:11-32), which violates family tradition; "The Banquet" (Matthew 22:1-14, Luke 14:15-24), to which the invited guests do not come. So "the poor, the crippled, the blind, and the lame" (Luke 14:21) are invited, "both good and bad." (Matthew 22:10) Everyone, without exception, may come.

Love neighbour and self

When asked, "Which commandment is the first of all?" Jesus summed up the requirements of living in God's realm by repeat-

ing the Old Testament injunctions to "love the Lord your God with
all your heart, and with all your soul, and with all your mind, and
with all your strength," and "You shall love your neighbour as
yourself." (Mark 12:28-31) He concludes, "On these two com-
mandments hang all the law and the prophets" (Matthew 22:40),
which means that life is about serving the Eros of the universe,
which shines in my neighbour and is the truth of my own soul.

In fact, everything is secondary to seeking this realm of God's
reign. "Strive first for the kingdom of God . . . and all these things
[food, shelter, clothing, family, the normal good things of life]
will be given to you as well." (Matthew 6:33) Everything must be
sacrificed, to buy this "one pearl of great value" (Matthew 13:45),
or to buy the field containing this treasure. (Matthew 13:44)

The realm of God surrounds us. It is not something far off and
distant. "The kingdom of God is among you" (Luke 17:21) in the
ordinary round of our daily living. Whenever and wherever we
experience love, we live within God's realm (kingdom).

Living in love results in abundance and blessing. Jesus said,
"I came that they may have life, and have it abundantly." (John
10:10b)

Jesus turned our usual values on their head by saying that blessing belongs to the poor in spirit, those who mourn, the meek, those
who hunger and thirst for righteousness, the merciful, the pure in
heart, the peacemakers, and those who are persecuted for righteousness' sake, and "you, when people revile you and persecute
you and utter all kinds of evil against you falsely on my account."
(Matthew 5:1-11)

In a power-seeking world, who honours the meek? In a pleas-
ure-seeking world, who will endure being reviled and persecuted?
Yet, according to Jesus' teaching, only through delving deeply into
the real experience of living will we find blessing and abundance.

The model of lived love

The writer of John's gospel presents Jesus as a model of love. He
writes, "This is my commandment, that you love one another as I
have loved you." (John 15:12)

We must love as he loved. But emulating his way is hard, especially when we consider where it led him. We know that Jesus' way leads to life, but having the integrity and courage to live it can be costly. Internally, it will bring peace and blessing, but it carries no guarantee of external blessing. The principalities and powers of this world are no more ready to stand under the glaring light of truth today than they were in Jesus' time. So more likely we will face some kind of a cross; we will pay a price for our integrity.

No, Jesus' teaching is not easy, but hearing it keeps us facing the truth of our own life and world. Jesus made love the core of life and put the pressure on us to do the same: "Do this, and you will live." (Luke 10:28)

Reflection questions

1. Think upon good teachers you have had. What qualities did they embody?
2. In what ways have you succeeded and failed in loving yourself?
3. In the "global village," who is your neighbour?

Your thoughts

31
The Jesus Seminar
(Perspectives On Jesus' Teaching)

O dear! You've heard of the Jesus Seminar and here I am quoting Jesus left and right as if he had actually said all those things!

The Jesus Seminar is a group of New Testament scholars (which started with 30 and eventually has involved more than 200) who have been meeting twice a year since 1985 to sort out which words attributed to Jesus he actually said.

Red beads!

No doubt they have lively discussions. For voting, they use coloured beads. Black means "no"; grey means "no, but the ideas are close"; pink means "probably"; and red means "for sure." The results show that these scholars agree that we cannot be absolutely sure that Jesus actually said most of the words attributed to him.

That very few words get the red-bead treatment disturbs some.

Not surprisingly, the Seminar has been roundly criticized. When we hear something we do not want to hear, our first impulse is to "shoot the messenger." These, however, are reputable scholars doing their thing. Their life work is examining the gospels and all relevant materials. They are not above criticism, but we need to pay attention to what they say.

These scholars expose themselves to criticism because they know the importance of making the fruits of their labours public. Some attack them for undermining our faith by casting doubt upon the Bible and the words of Jesus. But for many others the opposite happens. They find new and relevant meaning in Jesus and his teaching. They are part of the rising interest in Jesus, both in the church and the general public. We must thank the Seminar for providing scholarly information in a way we can understand.

The quest for the historical Jesus

They are reviving the old "quest for the historical Jesus." Last

century, when the modern methods of biblical criticism first burst
on the scene, there was a keen interest in finding the real Jesus
behind the writings. Albert Schweitzer was the best known propo-
nent of this process. That search more or less ended in failure. The
person of Jesus, scholars concluded, was lost in the murky mists
of the past. Better to focus on the Christ of faith than waste time
searching for the elusive Jesus of history.

Our modern world, however, will not leave Jesus alone. In the
general search for spiritual depth and meaning, the figure of Jesus
continues to intrigue. Andrew Lloyd Webber, in *Jesus Christ, Su-
perstar,* posed the question as well as anyone. He has the chorus
ask "Jesus Christ, Jesus Christ, Who are you? What have you sacrificed?" He has Judas saying, "Don't get me wrong. I only want
to know."

The Jesus Seminar, in trying to answer that question, shares
with us what can be known of Jesus' words from the available
texts. (And they basically use the four biblical gospels plus the
Gospel of Thomas, a Gnostic gospel that did not make it into the
official scriptures.) In this way, they help us develop an attitude
and approach to scripture that frees us from the literal words and
helps us see and feel the reality of the person behind the text. They
are doing what the original "quest" set out to do.

Playing with coloured beads is only part of what they do.

Some of them write books. They include Marcus J. Borg,
Meeting Jesus Again for the First Time; John Dominic Crossan,
Jesus: A Revolutionary Biography; and Robert W. Funk, *Honest
to Jesus, Jesus for a New Millennium.* The result of their work is
published in *The Five Gospels, With New Translation and Commentary,* by Robert W. Funk, Roy W. Hoover, and The Jesus Seminar.

Instead of receding into oblivion, Jesus is being presented in
lively and fresh ways.

The impact of Jesus

What emerges is the overwhelmingly powerful impact of the person Jesus.

We should have known this all along, but, as with Jesus' teaching, we have become immune. Think about it. Not many people have had the years counted from the date of their birth. A new religion does not start from nothing. The existence of the Christian church, in spite of all its faults and limitations, bears witness to a powerful presence that continues. Every word of the New Testament, plus many other gospels and writings, was written because of Jesus. The impact of Jesus has been a major founding and forming force of western civilization. The Judeo-Christian mythology, centred in the person of Jesus, is the undergirding myth of the whole western world.

The reality is that a man living two thousand years ago in the boondocks of Palestine is the pivotal figure of our world.

Does it really matter that we don't have many of Jesus' exact words?

Considering how the New Testament came into being, how could it be otherwise? Everything written was filtered through the mind and understanding of Jesus' followers. Every writer remembered Jesus' words through the lens of their own particular vision and understanding. Even the earliest gospel, Mark, was written about 35 years after Jesus' death. You can imagine what happens to exact words over that period of time.

The words may not be exact, but because of his impact as a person, the images and thoughts would be remembered. Jesus must have said something like what is recorded, and certainly words of equal power. We have more than we need to understand his mind and heart.

So I will continue to quote many of the words attributed to Jesus (at least the red and pink ones) knowing that, even if they are not exactly as he uttered them, they convey the power of his message and person.

What do we do with the words? To quote Shakespeare out of context, "The fault, dear Brutus, is not in our [words], But in ourselves"[1]. We must use scholarship to know all we can about Jesus and his words, but then we must allow those words to do their transforming work in us.

Reflection questions

1. Are you in the process of "meeting Jesus again for the first time," and if you are, what is different this time?
2. What "words" of Jesus have special power for you?
3. What do you think of the Jesus Seminar's way of sorting out what Jesus really said?

Your thoughts

32
The women in his life
(The Gospels)

Jesus had some very wholesome relationships with women. The gospels give us glimpses of a number of these women, and several of them were named Mary – a very common name in those days!

Mary, his mother

Mary, his mother was, of course, the first and undoubtedly the most important influence on him.

The birth accounts, being mostly later mythology, provide little help in knowing anything about her. We are left wondering: what songs did she sing to him, what stories did she tell him, and how did she care for him on a daily basis? "Mary's Song" (Luke 1:46-55) is a reworking of Hannah's Song (1 Samuel 2:1-10) by the early church, but may reflect something of Mary. Did Jesus hear from an early age about bringing down the powerful from their thrones, and lifting up the lowly; or filling the hungry with good things and sending the rich away empty?

In Jesus' adult years, we meet Mary as the mother of a large and well-known family. The neighbours, shocked by the words and actions of a local boy, wondered, "Where did this man get this wisdom and these deeds of power? Is not this the carpenter's son? Is not his mother called Mary? And are not his brothers James and Joseph and Simon and Judas? And are not all his sisters with us?" (Matthew 13:54b-56)

Jesus' mother figures prominently in "a wedding in Cana of Galilee." (John 2:1) The account begins by saying that "the mother of Jesus was there." (John 2:1b) She seems to be the hostess, which would explain her concern when the wine runs out — which brings up interesting questions about whose wedding this is! At least Jesus and his mother seem to have an easy relationship. She has every confidence that he will solve the wine problem, so she tells the servants, "Do whatever he tells you." (John 2:5)

But at some point a rift occurred between Jesus and his family. When he went to his hometown, even though the people thronged to him, the rumour was going around that "He has gone out of his mind." Mark tells us, "When his family heard it, they went out to restrain him." (Mark 3:21) They too, contrary to the birth myths, had to learn who he was. When told "Your mother and your brothers and sisters are outside, asking for you" (Mark 3:32b), his reply was, "Whoever does the will of God is my brother and sister and mother." (Mark 3:34b) He was affirming that there are things more important than the biological relationship.

The rift, however, was eventually healed, for we find Mary at the cross, and we know his brothers, especially James, played a major role in the early church. John's gospel reports a touching incident involving his mother. "Standing near the cross of Jesus were his mother, and his mother's sister, Mary the wife of Clopas, and Mary Magdalene. When Jesus saw his mother and the disciple whom he loved standing beside her, he said to his mother, 'Woman, here is your son.' Then he said to the disciple, 'Here is your mother.' And from that hour the disciple took her into his own home." (John 19:25b-27)

Jesus had female as well as male disciples, although the culture of the time limited the roles they could play. From the above quote, we can see that there were a number of women at the cross. Some are named, with obvious problems sorting out all the Marys. "These used to follow him and provide for him when he was in Galilee; and there were many other women who had come up with him to Jerusalem." (Mark 15:41)

Women were among his constant followers. It would be interesting to know more about them and the role they played.

Mary Magdalene

The most elusive, and perhaps the most significant, woman in Jesus' life was one of this band of female disciples, Mary Magdalene.

We know little about her, only that she was from Magdala and that "seven demons had gone out" (Luke 8:2b) of her. Every time, save in the above John quote, her name comes first when the women are listed. The longer ending of Mark says that "he [Jesus] appeared first to Mary Magdalene." (Mark 16:9) In John's gospel, she comes alone to the tomb and meets the risen Jesus. (John 20:1,11-18) She must have been the leading female disciple and a special companion to Jesus. Bishop Spong, in *Born of a Woman*, makes a case for her being Jesus' wife!

The early church, unable to cope with a sexually powerful woman, tagged her as a prostitute. Whatever the sexual arrangements, she obviously belonged to the inner circle of Jesus' intimates and was very important to him.

Mary and Martha

Mary and Martha were special friends of Jesus. He probably made their home his headquarters when visiting Judea. He related to each quite differently. Martha, the hostess, "welcomed him into her home" (Luke 10:38), but then became annoyed when her sister Mary left her to do all the work. Mary "sat at the Lord's feet and listened to what he was saying." (Luke 10:39) The gospel writer has Jesus say that "Mary has chosen the better part" (Luke 10:42), but I suspect the tradition played up the image of quiet, docile, female piety to suit the patriarchy already growing in the church.

Martha, in John's gospel, is the first to understand that Jesus is the Christ (John 11:27), although we hear much less of Martha's "confession" than of Peter's! Her "confession" comes at the end of a theological discussion surrounding the death of Lazarus, brother of Martha and Mary. On the same occasion, when Mary meets Jesus, their conversation has a more emotional tone which culminates with Jesus weeping.

At a later time they "gave a dinner for [Jesus]." Typically, "Martha served." (John 12:2) Mary, on the other hand, "took a pound of costly perfume, . . . anointed Jesus' feet, and wiped them with her hair." (John 12:3) It takes little imagination to feel the sexual electricity in this intimate act. Whatever else, it is a powerful symbolic act of her caring.

The Martha/Mary/Lazarus home must have been an oasis for Jesus. In these scenes, we find him nourishing and being nourished by these remarkable women.

The women surrounding Jesus give us a picture of the wholeness and fullness of his life. All the more reason why we can relate to him, knowing he understands and affirms us in the midst of our daily living.

Reflection questions

1. Do the tensions within Jesus' parental home caused by him following his own path reflect anything of your experience?
2. Do your same sex, opposite sex, and lesbian-gay friendships differ, and if so in what ways?
3. Can you imagine Jesus being married?

Your thoughts

33
The women he meets
(The Gospels)

Jesus' disciples, returning from grocery shopping, "were astonished that he was speaking with a woman." (John 4:27) That about
sums up the general attitude toward women during the latter part
of the first century, when these words were penned.

It also tells us that Jesus broke the conventions of his day and
dealt with women normally and naturally as full persons. A few
incidents should firmly fix this simple truth in our minds.

The woman at the well

The scene I've pictured is doubly surprising because the woman is
a Samaritan, and "the Jews have no dealings with the Samaritans."
(John 4:9b KJV) The image of Jesus talking with a Samaritan
woman captures his inclusive attitude toward women, Samaritans,
or whoever crossed his path.

We would not expect to find Jesus travelling through Samaria.
True, it lay between Galilee and Judea, the natural route for anyone making that journey. Jews, however, abhorred Samaritans, so
they would cross the Jordan to avoid going through the country of
these "impure apostates." Such niceties obviously did not bother
Jesus.

Jesus and the woman were having a profound discussion on
the Jew/Samaritan issue. After Jesus related intimate details of her
life to her, she said, "Sir, I see that you are a prophet. Our ancestors worshipped on this mountain, but you say that the place where
people must worship is in Jerusalem." (John 4:19-20) Here was an
intelligent and perceptive Samaritan woman having a theological
conversation with a Jewish man. This was unheard of. Not much
wonder the disciples were astonished.

The gentile woman

On another occasion, during a northern excursion outside of Jewish territory, Jesus had his vision broadened by a local woman.

Jesus "did not want anyone to know he was there." (Mark 7:24) He needed some time away from the public eye and with his disciples. No doubt he was annoyed when (shifting to Matthew's account) "a Canaanite woman from that region came out and started shouting, 'Have mercy on me, Lord, Son of David; my daughter is tormented by a demon.' But he did not answer her at all." (Matthew 15:22-23a)

The disciples urged him to "send her away, for she keeps shouting after us." (Matthew 15:23b) Jesus found an excuse in his belief that he was "sent only to the lost sheep of the house of Israel." (Matthew 15:24) He expressed this attitude by telling her, "It is not fair to take the children's food and throw it to the dogs." (Matthew 15:26) But the woman was not put off by the insulting statement. She responded, "Even the dogs eat the crumbs." (Matthew 15:27)

Some interpret this as humorous banter. I think, however, that Jesus was simply caught at a bad moment. When the woman confronts him, we can almost see him suddenly snap out of his weariness and insular attitude and really become aware of her. Now he responds person to person: "Woman, great is your faith! Let it be done for you as you wish." (Matthew 15:28) Jesus allowed a foreign woman to teach him, and he honoured her for her confident faith.

A desperate woman

"A woman who had been suffering from haemorrhages" (Mark 5:25) approached Jesus more subtly. She had been ill for years and had run the gamut of doctors, but only "grew worse. She had heard about Jesus, and [desperate to be healed] came up behind him in the crowd and touched his cloak. . . Immediately her haemorrhage stopped; and she felt in her body that she was healed of her disease." (Mark 5:26b-29)

Jesus, caught by surprise, stopped. "Immediately aware that power had gone forth from him," he asked, "Who touched my clothes?" (Mark 5:30) The disciples scoffed, since the crowd was pressing in on all sides. Jesus would not be put off, and "looked all around to see who had done it." (Mark 5:32)

The woman, probably shocked by her own audacity, knew the jig was up. She "came in fear and trembling, fell down before him, and told him the whole truth." (Mark 5:33) But Jesus was not angry with her. He simply wanted to honour her for her courageous faith, so told her, "Daughter, your faith has made you well; go in peace, and be healed of your disease." (Mark 5:34)

The woman caught in adultery

The moralistic ones thought they had Jesus trapped. They thrust before him a woman caught in adultery. (It takes two to tango; where was the man?) "And making her stand before all of them [sans clothes?], they said to him . . . 'Moses commanded us to stone such women. Now what do you say?'" (John 8:3-5)

"Jesus bent down and wrote with his finger on the ground" (John 8:6b) — the only reference to Jesus writing anything. Was he embarrassed? Was he playing for time? They kept badgering him, and eventually he straightened up and gave the classic line, "Let anyone among you who is without sin be the first to throw a stone at her." (John 8:7)

"When they heard it, they went away, one by one." (John 8:9) Finally, Jesus was left alone with the woman. He "said to her, 'Woman, where are they? Has no one condemned you?' She said, 'No one, sir.' And Jesus said, 'Neither do I condemn you'." (John 8:11)

That was a different approach that must have baffled those who heard it.

A Prostitute who anointed Jesus

Then there is the anointing incident. In John's gospel, Mary of Mary and Martha does it. The other gospels have different versions.

In Luke, it happens at the home of Simon, who is a Pharisee. "A woman in the city, who was a sinner [prostitute] . . . brought an alabaster jar of ointment. She stood behind him at his feet, weeping, and began to bathe his feet with her tears and to dry them with her hair. Then she continued kissing his feet and anointing them with the ointment." (Luke 7:37-38)

This woman must have seen in Jesus one who accepted her and affirmed her worth. That she would venture into the home of a Pharisee is amazing. That she would so lavishly express her affection, which must have had sexual overtones for both, was astounding. Obviously, women would break taboos to get to Jesus, and Jesus would do the same to respond as one human being to another.

Jesus and women

From these few glimpses of Jesus and women, which represent either actual happenings or the later understanding of the gospel writers, we can see that he accepted women and dealt with them in the same way he would deal with men. It is hard for us to realize the total novelty of Jesus' approach in the world of his day.

Still today, Jesus stands as a model and a challenge as we strive toward the equality of women and men.

Reflection questions

1. In what ways does gender influence your relationships with others?
2. What qualities do you see in Jesus' ability to cut across sexual, social, ethnic, and seemingly all boundaries?
3. How does society reflect, and fail to reflect, Jesus as a model for our relationships?

Your thoughts

34
Testing his integrity
(Matthew 26:36-46; Mark 14:32-42; Luke 22:39-46)

Integrity is being out there in the world as who you truly are — not always a comfortable situation.

Life brings integrity-testing moments. For Jesus, the Garden of Gethsemane was such a one. At that point death faced him. The full consequence of his life and mission became clear to him, and he had to make a decision. Would he go to his death in service of his mission or flee to safer ground and live to fight another day?

He had accepted his destiny at his baptism. From then on, he spent his life calling people to look into the mirror of their own lives and to live the radical integrity which he practised. Some liked it. Some didn't.

Calling to integrity

Calling people to integrity can be dangerous, a fact which Jesus learned early.

He had returned to his home community, Nazareth. The first response to his speaking in the synagogue was typical "hometown boy made good." Luke 4:22 says, "All spoke well of him and were amazed at the gracious words that came from his mouth." But when he went on to say, in effect, "You're not listening, folks," they responded differently. When he went a step farther and made clear that, if they did not listen, others outside the faith would, they took action. "When they heard this, all in the synagogue were filled with rage," (Luke 4:28) and drove him out of town with the intent of hurling him off a cliff.

Confronting the rage of a crowd requires a high degree of inner strength and security. "But he passed through the midst of them and went on his way." (Luke 4:30) Perhaps the intensity of his integrity broke through their rage and stopped them in their tracks.

150   CELEBRATING EVE

Calling institutions to integrity is even more hazardous.

I am awed by the care Jesus took in setting up his final confrontation with his country's political and religious powers. According
to the outline of his life given to us by Mark, and more or less
repeated in Matthew and Luke, Jesus carefully avoided meeting
his end in the boondocks, where it would go unnoticed.

When he had met dangerous opposition, he escaped by taking
a tour northward, outside of Jewish territory. He needed time to
make sure that the disciples had some grasp of who he was.before
returning to the south, he asked them, "Who do you say that I
am?" It was then the truth dawned on Peter causing him to ex-
claim "You are the Messiah." (Mark 8:29)

Jesus tried, unsuccessfully, to explain that being the Messiah
would bring suffering and death. The idea of a suffering Messiah
proved too much for the disciples to grasp; after all, a Messiah
was supposed to be a strong, tough leader, not a victim. They could
understand only after living through it. So, "He set his face to go
to Jerusalem." (Luke 9:51)

Entering Jerusalem

The moment was right. Large numbers were gathering for the
Passover feast. Messiah fever crackled through the crowd. Jesus
took full advantage of the situation by making a carefully planned
appearance riding on a donkey. This symbolic act announced pub-
licly that here is the Messiah. Their tradition told them, "Lo, your
king comes to you; triumphant and victorious is he, humble and
riding on a donkey." (Zechariah 9:9) And there he was, before
their eyes. "The whole city was in turmoil, asking, 'Who is this?'"
(Matthew 21:10)

Like all oppressive governments, the Romans feared large
crowds. A crowd could easily get out of hand. Patrols no doubt
quickly reported the incident and kept a nervous watch.

As if that wasn't enough, Jesus "entered the temple and began
to drive out those who were selling and those who were buying in
the temple, and he overturned the tables of the money changers
and the seats of those who sold doves." (Mark 11:15)

It is hard for us to imagine either the intense righteous anger of Jesus or the affront his actions caused the authorities. "And when the chief priests and the scribes heard it, they kept looking for a way to kill him; for they were afraid of him, because the whole crowd was spellbound by his teaching." (Mark 11:18)

Jesus had succeeded in challenging both the political and religious authorities. They responded as institutions will, by doing whatever is necessary to get rid of the irritant.

Jesus and his disciples would be feeling the pressure. In this tense atmosphere, they gathered for the Passover meal. There Jesus instituted the Eucharist ritual by breaking the bread and passing the cup, as symbols of his life and impending death. Judas cracked under the strain, and off he went to betray Jesus.

Gethsemane

There was now no escape. "When they had sung the hymn, they went out to the Mount of Olives," (Mark 14:26) and then on to Gethsemane.

We can know something with our heads long before it penetrates to the core of our being. Jesus had intimations right from the beginning that his ministry would end with his death. Now the handwriting was on the wall. He "began to be grieved and agitated. . . . And going a little farther, he threw himself on the ground and prayed, 'My Father, if it is possible, let this cup pass from me; yet not what I want but what you want'." (Matthew 26:37b,39) "And his sweat became like great drops of blood falling down on the ground." (Luke 22:44b)

Jesus could accept death no more easily than any of us. His own human ego self wanted out. The price he now had to pay for his integrity was far too high! Three times he prayed, returning each time to his sleeping disciples. Each time, the same answer came to him: "Not my will but yours be done." (Luke 22:42b)

The little self serves the big self

Until we come to maturity, our little ego selves and our big self will struggle for supremacy. Fear and possibility contend. Following the call of the soul, or of God, usually comes at a cost. Not always are we prepared to pay it.

In Gethsemane, we have a classic model of the inner struggle in which ego finally agrees to serve the big self — life's purpose, or God. Here, revealed in stark clarity, is the call to be out in the world in the fullness of our integrity.

In this sense, we are called to do the will of God.

Reflection questions

1. Think of some major tests to your integrity. What was the test, and how did you respond?
2. What are some of the little, perhaps daily, tests to your integrity?
3. What are some blocks to your being your full self in the world?

Your thoughts

35
Forsaken
(Mark 15:33-39; Matthew 27:45-54)

Of the traditional "seven words from the cross" attributed to Jesus, six are very appropriate and Jesus-like.

Luke reports three of them. "Father, forgive them; for they do not know what they are doing, (Luke 23:34) a suitable word to those crucifying him. To the men crucified on either side of him, Jesus said, "Truly I tell you, today you will be with me in Paradise." (Luke 23:43) Jesus died with the words, "Father, into your hands I commend my spirit." (Luke 23:46) What could be more fitting?

John also has three, different from Luke. When Jesus saw his mother he said, "Woman, here is your son," and to "the disciple, 'Here is your mother'." (John 19:26-27) Jesus, the loving son, makes sure his mother will be looked after. Then Jesus said, "I am thirsty" (John 19:28) — a touch of humanity. After receiving some wine on a sponge he died with the words, "It is finished." (John 19:30) Again, these are words in keeping with Jesus' character.

Both these accounts leave us with the feeling that Jesus died as we would expect him to die.

Jarring words

Mark and Matthew give us the jarring utterance: "Eloi, Eloi, lema sabachthani?" which means, "My God, my God, why have you forsaken me?" (Mark 15:34) Some think he is calling for Elijah, but, after being given some sour wine on a sponge, "Jesus gave a loud cry and breathed his last." (Mark 15:37)

Jesus' cry seems out of place and out of character. We expect something "better" of a person of such quality. Mark and Matthew report no other words, and add to the starkness of his death by having him die with an anguished yell.

When I read this, I get a glimpse of the loneliness, the anguish and pain, the utter desolate abandonment, that Jesus must have felt. He neither received or gave any reassuring words. The Presence, with whom he had all along communed as with a loving parent, had vanished, gone, was not to be found.

Some commentators attempt to take the edge off his cry by suggesting that Jesus was quoting Psalm 22, which begins with the words Jesus uttered but ends with a great burst of hope. To believe that Jesus gave voice to these words of forsakenness while thinking of hope is a long stretch. If he wanted to express hope, why did he not quote Psalm 23: "The Lord is my shepherd"?

I believe that Jesus meant exactly what he said. The fact that these are not the words we expect adds authenticity. It is unlikely that anyone would make them up. And Mark, being the earliest gospel, has the best chance of being authentic.

To know the full depths of Jesus' human experience, we must look, unflinchingly, into his final words.

Ultimate loneliness

Loneliness is probably the most painful and universal human experience. We have all known it. People die; marriages end; friendships cool.

On the cross, Jesus knew ultimate loneliness. Only the women (and one account adds "friends") stood at a distance, helplessly watching. When the crunch came, his disciples abandoned him. The crowds, who so recently were shouting "Hosanna" in his honour, had turned against him and clamoured for his death. Not even his disciples seemed to grasp the purpose of his life. Again and again, he had tried to warn them of what was coming, but they didn't get it. He must have felt a total failure.

Jesus experienced the most common, yet ultimate, consequence of the dark side of the journey to consciousness. The full weight of the loneliness we experience when we step into consciousness descended on him. He had no one with whom to share his level of awareness and maturity. Totally alone, he experienced the darkness of a world far from wholeness.

His ultimate suffering was to feel abandoned by God. The oneness that he had known with his God had vanished. All the times he had sorted out the course of his life as he communed with the great Mystery, whom he experienced as "Abba" (beloved parent), was now of no avail. His life must have seemed a hopeless mistake.

On the reasons behind Jesus' cry of desolation we can only speculate. Perhaps his own image of God needed a reality check. In the fray of his capture, when someone had drawn a sword, Jesus had said, "Put your sword back into its place . . . . Do you think that I cannot appeal to my Father, and he will at once send me more than twelve legions of angels?" (Matthew 26:52-53) Apparently Jesus believed that God could send angels, but no angels came. God did not come to his rescue. Jesus was left to bear the full power of evil, the consequences of messiahship, by himself.

Jesus died, according to the earliest accounts, knowing only that God had not come. In the fullness of his humanity, knowing the ultimate terror of loneliness, failure, abandonment, and nothingness, "Jesus gave a loud cry and breathed his last." (Mark 15:37)

To heal the wound

In order to heal the wound of consciousness, the inner separation that happens when we become conscious, Jesus had to experience the ultimate abyss of our separation from our essence, from love, from God. He had to be "made . . . sin who knew no sin." (2 Corinthians 5:21)

This experience imprinted the collective unconscious, the heavenly realm, Yahweh, with a purifying and wholing power that is still at work. It opened the way for resurrection, the Holy Spirit, and the ultimate wedding of heaven and earth in the just and loving community of the New Jerusalem.

Can we too allow the light of truth to shine upon us, live with the integrity of who we are, face the powers of darkness in the world and within ourselves, and pay whatever price we need to pay?

When we do, resurrection will happen.

Reflection questions

1. Reflect on times in your life when you have felt most alone. What helped you to get through such times?
2. Have there been ways in which your experience, or that of people you know, reflects something of Jesus experience of being abandoned when he took the ultimate step of integrity?
3. What usually happens when someone exposes wrong-doing?

Your thoughts

36
Resurrection
(Matthew 28; Mark 16; Luke 24; John 20-21)

Resurrection is not about a dead body getting up and walking around again. It is about the reality that "truth crushed to the earth will rise again." (Martin Luther King Jr.) Nothing supernatural or unnatural is at work. Resurrection is the natural and normal way life works.

Resurrection means that what we are lives on after us. How we express that, or what it means in detail, is explained in many ways but ultimately resides in the Mystery of being. I venture a few words.

Jesus' resurrection means that who Jesus was, the energy and content of his life, remained active and alive after his physical death. Because Jesus had a very special role to play, and seems to have fulfilled it rather well, examining how his resurrection was, and is, experienced may help us understand all resurrection.

The fact of Jesus' resurrection cannot be denied. Everything I have said about the impact of Jesus' life applies also to his resurrection. The disciples' experience of Jesus' resurrection transformed them, resurrected them. In the power of the resurrection, they and their followers became the church and made Christianity the undergirding mythology of the western world.

We know that something powerful happened, but the particulars of exactly what happened and how it happened present more of a problem.

The empty tomb

Many scholars now doubt the empty tomb tradition. It may have been made up to counter the rumour that the disciples had stolen the body. (Matthew 28:11-15) Mark used it, and the other gospel writers may have simply copied it, adding the traditions that they knew.

The story shows the normal signs of having grown with the telling. All the writers agree that Mary Magdalene, either alone

(John) or with others, came to the tomb early Sunday morning. Who did she see there? In Mark, "they saw a young man, dressed in a white robe." (Mark 16:5) In Matthew, the young man becomes an angel whose "appearance was like lightning, and his clothing white as snow." (Matthew 28:3) In Luke, "Suddenly two men in dazzling clothes stood beside them." (Luke 24:4) And in John, Mary Magdalene "saw two angels in white." (John 20:12)

Even though the details vary and are embellished with the passage of time, I believe there is some reality behind the empty tomb tradition. I hang that belief on a couple of things.

Young man in a white robe

First is the thin thread of the "young man, dressed in a white robe," of Mark's gospel. In recounting the capture of Jesus, mark records this interesting detail: "A certain young man was following him, wearing nothing but a linen cloth. They caught hold of him, but he left the linen cloth and ran off naked." (Mark 14:51)

Why include this detail? It seems to serve no purpose, and Mark otherwise wasted few words in writing his gospel. Could he be talking about himself? There is a tradition that the upper room, where Jesus and his disciples gathered for their last supper, belonged to Mark's mother. Perhaps Mark, a normal nosey teenager, was hanging around and followed them to the garden, where in the ensuing fracas he lost his meagre clothing. Could this same young man, still dressed in night attire, still nosey, have sneaked off to the tomb and been there to greet the women when they arrived? Perhaps Mark was describing something he knew first-hand.

My other argument involves the change in the day of worship from Saturday to Sunday. The Jewish Sabbath was Saturday. The Christians chose to worship on Sunday. Something traumatic must have happened on Sunday to cause that change.

Appearance in Galilee

I believe that something major happened on Sunday, but apparently it did not immediately convince the disciples. They, for whatever reasons, went off to Galilee. Perhaps they were following instructions. In Mark, the young man hears the message to "tell his disciples and Peter that he is going ahead of you to Galilee; there you will see him." (Mark 16:7) Matthew repeats the same message. (Matthew 28:7) Luke has no Galilee tradition, but John's final chapter tells of a Galilean meeting. Perhaps Galilee was the location of the most powerful resurrection appearance. For a full discussion read Bishop Spong's *Resurrection: Myth or Reality.*

Whatever happened, the disciples' awareness that Jesus was alive became a conviction deeper than words or rational thought. They had been despondent men returning to the work they knew: "Peter said to them, 'I am going fishing'. They said to him, 'We will go with you'." (John 21:3) They were transformed into passionate and convincing apostles who went out to begin "turning the world upside down." (Acts 17:6b)

The messiah archetype

What we know about archetypes is relevant here. The messiah archetype, which in some sense brought forth Jesus, would be transformed and focused by his life. With his death, the archetypal energy which he had embodied would become available among his followers.

The writer of John's gospel, after many years of reflection on the life, death, and resurrection of Jesus, has Jesus explain it by saying, "It is to your advantage that I go away, for if I do not go away, the Advocate will not come to you. . . . When the Spirit of truth comes, he will guide you into all the truth." (John 16:7,13) The Advocate, the Holy Spirit, whom the Father will send in my name, will teach you everything, and remind you of all that I have said to you." (John 14:26) The Christ energy, shaped and strengthened by Jesus' life, returns with renewed power as the Holy Spirit released into the world.

That this psychic energy could appear in the bodily form of Jesus may challenge our cynical scientific minds. Yet there is nothing strange about this. It fits the tradition of psychic appearances.

Ghosts, we are told, often appear where some issue or injustice has not been resolved at the time of the persons' death. It seems believable to me that such an event would leave a psychic mark, a ghost. Jesus' death was an ultimate injustice. The heavenly realm knew that a terrible injustice remained unresolved at Jesus' death. There was work to be done, which activates the Christ archetype. The psychic energy of Jesus' life could well appear and will continue at work until every wrong and injustice is healed and humanity comes to maturity.

Jesus' resurrection and ours

Jesus has given us a classic model of resurrection. Presumably life, death, and resurrection is the normal course life takes, which means that our lives will follow the same pattern. As we live authentically, we add our energies to the cosmic yearning that wants wholeness for all people and the entire world to be a realm of justice and peace. This energy appears as the Holy Spirit, our companion on the road to wholeness.

Resurrection is real. Believe it.

Reflection questions

1. Have you had any experience of psychic appearances (ghosts) and, if so, what did it meant for you?
2. How does understanding Jesus' resurrection as a natural aspect of life help you to understand how our individual lives are part of the whole of life? Or does it?
3. "What we do matters eternally." Do you believe that, and if so, what difference does it make?

Your thoughts

37
Yahweh's initiation
(Jesus' Life From Yahweh's Point Of View)

If Job caused Yahweh considerable consternation, think what Jesus did.

In the generations after Job, Yahweh's yearning to incarnate had grown — if we can read the emerging longing among the people for a Messiah as a reflection of the archetypal reality.

Of course, the information we have from the human side (the biblical account, even with all its problems) is much more complete than from the Yahweh side, which we have only by inference. I will simply give my imaginative view, reflecting Jung's understanding as well as I can, on how the dynamics of the heavenly/mythic realm works.

Yahweh becomes incarnated

Yahweh must have looked forward to incarnation with excitement and apprehension. On the one hand, incarnating within a human life was the next great step in Yahweh's growth. On the other hand, Yahweh would have to deal with a human being who had free will. That person could choose both whether or not to take on the messiah role and how to live it. Yahweh had no direct control, a situation that would cause most of us considerable anxiety.

The mythic realm, however, has many kinds of indirect influence. Yahweh must have nurtured the messiah yearning with great care. Developing a self, or soul, to carry the essence of Yahweh's own being would be a satisfying work of art. Jesus' birth would be a high point, but waiting for him to grow up and take on his assigned role must have been a nervous time.

Jesus' baptism was the decisive moment. There Jesus knew himself to be the Messiah, and Yahweh's delight burst forth in the words, "You are my Son, the Beloved; with you I am well pleased." (Mark 1:11) At last, Yahweh could live in Jesus.

A whole new experience

Being human, however, was a whole new ball game. Strangely, Yahweh had never before made the final leap. We can imagine that Yahweh knew humanity as we might know a friend. Our knowing is never complete. To fully know another person we would have to, in some sense, become that person. So, while still remaining the God-image of the mythic realm, Yahweh had to become human.

Yahweh had never before felt the warmth of the sun or the chill wind, never known hunger or thirst, never experienced the necessity to urinate and defecate. The urge to mate would be novel. Becoming aware of the immediacy of the cultural, religious, and political situation would take some getting used to. Within everything was the overwhelming necessity of getting on with being the Messiah, of living out the fullness of love within a human life.

Yahweh, as archetype, still could not act directly. It was up to the intelligence and depth of the human Jesus to carry out the task of being the human expression of Eros. The ego self of Jesus had to accept and work out what it meant to be the presence of Yahweh in the world. Yahweh, as the big self of Jesus, would have experienced the anxiety, frustrations, anger, and joy of coping with the human situation. Yahweh was on a steep learning curve.

Yahweh's delight

Overall, though, Yahweh took delight in the experience of being human. Yahweh's human self, Jesus, was doing very well.

Once, in a burst of insight and pride, Yahweh broke through as a mystical experience of the inner circle of disciples: Peter, James, and John. They were on the top of a high mountain with Jesus. Right there before their eyes, Jesus took on an ethereal appearance. Moses and Elijah joined this visionary scene, symbols of the long tradition that had gone before. Jesus was carrying forward that history. Yahweh burst forth with the words, very similar to the baptismal words, "This is my Son, the Beloved; listen to him!" (Mark 9:7)

The words, "Listen to him!" have an urgency. The weight of being human was descending on Yahweh. The ominous clouds gathered as Jesus headed for Jerusalem. Obviously, serious trouble awaited him. Yahweh now knew that this experiment in being human would end in tragedy.

These human creatures were slower learners than Yahweh had anticipated. Anger and intimidation had not changed them. Becoming a nation had not done it. Prophets had made some advances, but few people paid attention. Now Jesus was about to be killed. Yahweh must have wondered whether giving creatures free will and expecting them to become sufficiently mature to use it for their own good might be asking too much!

But there was no turning back. Having begun the experiment, it must be carried through. Being human was the final step Eros, through Yahweh, could take. If this didn't work, Eros would be left unpartnered and lonely. The very nature of Eros required that Yahweh give the human venture Yahweh's best shot.

Yahweh experiences death

Yahweh could only admire the way Jesus had set up the Jerusalem scenario. Both the political and religious authorities were being put to the test.

Yahweh would also experience anger and frustration. The people among whom Jesus lived, in order to avoid facing the truth of themselves, would extinguish the truth! How could these humans be so blind, stupid, incompetent, vindictive, and cruel? They were not created for this. The full-blown demonic power of the dark side of their immaturity was at work.

It all came to a head in the garden of Gethsemane. The whole incarnation experiment was on the line. Could Jesus take the final step and accept death? What relief and joy would come to Yahweh upon hearing the words, "Not what I want, but what you want." (Mark 14:36b) But the stark reality of what that meant must have immediately descended on Yahweh. This stage of the human experiment was ending. Yahweh must now give up life within a human and experience the anguish of abandonment and death.

Yahweh was shaken to the core.

Yahweh's own immaturity could not be ignored. The fits of anger, jealousy, fear, and petulance now came back to haunt Yahweh. Guilt, a new emotion, descended. Yahweh had to face the dark side within that was part of the darkness putting Jesus to death.

Yet Yahweh also had all the love and compassion that a parent feels for a child facing the pain of life and death. As archetype and human, Yahweh was both the subject and observer of Jesus' death. Yahweh had to both suffer crucifixion and watch the beloved one be crucified.

Jesus' final words, "My God, my God, why have you forsaken me?" (Mark 15:34), must have torn Yahweh apart. Yahweh had precipitated and was now experiencing the death of Jesus. The love and the demonic were both there. Yahweh had unknowingly and unintentionally sacrificed Yahweh's own incarnation, Jesus, to the human experiment; something that would bring any one of us to ultimate anguish.

A new longing

Now Yahweh knew the exhilaration, pain, and guilt of being fully human in an impure and imperfect world. I understand this a little through knowing the exhilaration, pain, and guilt of taking a step toward wholeness by ending a marriage. Knowing you share in the common glory and guilt of humanity, as Yahweh now did, creates a powerful bond with all the struggling lives of the world.

This dynamic, we can believe, created in Yahweh a new longing for full partnership with humanity. To satisfy that yearning, both Yahweh and humanity must now grow to the full maturity that Jesus possessed.

From Jesus' time on, the power of that awareness has been at work.

Reflection questions

1. Do these excursions into the being and dynamics of Yahweh help you understand the collective unconscious, the mythic realm, or leave you shaking your head?
2. Yahweh's adventure in getting to know humanity is a meta-

phor for the possibility of getting to know your real life self. What does your big self have to say to your here-and-now self, and vice versa?

3. How has your life been shaped by an experience of loss or tragedy?

Your thoughts

Note

1. Shakespeare, William. *Julius Caesar,* 1.I, 139-140

Humanity

It's Time

You sit cross legged at the Buddha's feet
You give your heart to Jesus cause you know he took the heat
You think about the eagle sitting up in the tree
you too see all the people who are yearning to be free

And you know it's time
You know it's time
For we've gone some thousand years
With our wars and with our fears
And we want for everyone (yes, we want for everyone)
No more tears, (no more tears)
no more (we don't need more) tears!

You stand in awe as the butterfly
wings its journey south and you suspect goodbye
You somehow know the panther and the flimsy moth
will also join the fate of that great long-gone giant sloth.

And you know it's time
You know it's time
For we've gone some thousand years
With our wars and with our fears
And we want for everything (yes, we want for everything)
No more tears, (no more tears)
no more (we don't need more) tears!

The sky at night is so full of stars
It can't reflect the earth, how we've inflicted scars
You pray to someone, somewhere, for perhaps it's come-
the time to heal the brokenness, a new millennium.

And you know it's time
You know it's time
We're in a brand new thousand years
With brilliant hopes and wounding fears
Now we want humanity (yes, we want humanity)
And Mother Earth, (and Mother Earth)
just to be (can you and me be?) free.

Emily Kierstead

38
Slow learners

(The biblical story)

To say that life is our school for learning does not condone all the suffering, torture, oppression, injustice, and death that are the reality of our present world and the stuff of history. It does say that humanity is far from wholeness because we are slow learners. Since Eve took the first step into awareness, history has been our school, and we learn the lessons of history slowly.

Why such slow learners?

Why we are such slow learners resides in the mystery, but we do have some clues.

We need look no farther than our own lives to know how difficult it is to change and grow. Unfortunately, we learn only by experience, and then only if we stop to think about it and make some decisions about how we will think and act differently.

Many things get in the way. Developing the discipline and skills to do whatever we need to do often takes more time and attention than we are prepared to give. The pianist has to spend considerable time learning the art and craft of playing. To use a computer to do this writing, I had to learn a little about how it works, and resist learning more than I need to.

Structuring our lives to have enough time for exercise, spiritual practices, partner, family, friends, work, community, church, myself, and whatever else, is a balancing act that, in my experience, is never totally achieved. My fantasy about retirement pictured lots of time to do everything I wanted and needed to do. But the lists just keep getting longer, and the basement still awaits.

There are also much deeper reasons for our slow learning.

Something in us seems to work against us. With Paul we can say, "I do not understand my own actions. For I do not do what I want, but I do the very thing I hate. . . . I can will what is right, but I cannot do it." (Romans 7: 15,18b)

Jung drew a distinction between the ego and the self. Some

169

people talk about the little self and the big self, or the actual self and the ideal self. However we word it, there seems to be a self that exists in this world and a self that exists in possibility or in the mythic realm, and they are often at odds with one another — if they pay any attention to one another at all.

Yet my purpose in life is to incarnate my possible self. It seems simple enough, so why am I so slow at getting on with it?

Fear

Fear is the culprit.

Fear comes quickly into my life. I start life with a very limited awareness of myself or the world about me. Lots of people and forces out there quickly tell me who I should be and what I should do. "Should's" come at me from every side, and they awaken fear. Eventually, out of some inner awareness of who I am and the demands of the world around me, I cobble together some kind of identity. But it is very tenuous and fragile.

Our little egos, afloat on the great sea of life, have much to fear. We can fear parents, people, the world, the boss, our inner demons, the "enemy." We fear our possibilities. We fear the unknown future. Ultimately, we fear death and nothingness.

We tend to cling to our ego selves as to a lifeboat. Much of our energy goes into protecting our incomplete and fragile egos rather than venturing out into the unknown. Freedom is awesome and fearful. For the Israelites at the time of the Exodus, Egypt represented security, but the price was slavery. Many wanted to return even after venturing into freedom. How many forms of slavery do we choose rather than taking the risk of leaving our secure world and venturing into the unknown?

Because of our fear, psychology tells us, we build a whole set of neuroses and complexes to protect ourselves against the unknown. Someone has likened these neuroses to the bars of a jail that keep us imprisoned but secure. We tend to cling to bad habits, outdated beliefs, destructive ways of relating, a job that fails to challenge us, a bad marriage, or an unhealthy situation, long after we know better. Look at how many still smoke! I'm supposed to eat the right things to keep my cholesterol and blood pressure down, but it isn't easy.

We construct our society to reflect our inner world, prisons and all. We do it so well that, as I have read somewhere, any institution which evolves to meet a need will end up blocking that need. I don't totally believe that — institutions can evolve. But many say that institutional religion blocks the spirit; that education stifles creativity; that the justice system can be unjust; that the medical establishment limits healing.

In our messed-up world, that which carries the light also carries the darkness.

Hope for growth

All is not lost. The call of life continually urges us on. At an elemental level, we want to remain alive and be happy.

We quickly learn that we live among people. We want our families, communities, countries, etc., to be places of security and peace. Slowly, we learn that good community requires justice, compassion, and humility. (Micah 6:8)

We feel deeply called to serve the community. We find ways of using our unique gifts and opportunities to serve the community. Actually, all authentic life serves the community.

In the process, we find personal fulfilment and enhance our common life. We hope that over the years our awareness of self and world deepens and our ability to be our true selves in the world grows.

Fear recedes, and the ego and the self find more and more ways to co-operate.

Some want to get rid of the ego since, being self-centred, it seems to get in the way. But we are stuck with our ego, whether we like it or not. It is the centre of our conscious selves, the only carrier we have for the big self.

Our ego must become strong enough to cast aside our fears and move beyond our self- centred existence and become the servants of our big selves, which ultimately means serving God and humanity. We must grow until our will mirrors God's will for us. I have tried to show that Eve, Job, and Jesus each represent stages of a growing inner strength. Humanity as a whole must now develop the same inner authority as Jesus.

There is, however, many a slip between the cup and the lip, many casualties along the way. After the Exodus, many people died in the wilderness. We hope that humanity is not the ultimate casualty.

The struggle between fear and possibility goes on. It is the whole story of the Bible, our lives, and human history, and ultimately of the universe and God. In spite of how slowly we learn, may it ever be a story of hope.

Reflection questions

1. What must western society learn if we are to survive?
2. What blocks to change do you meet at work, home, community, church, country?
3. What within yourself resists changes you should make and how do you overcome them?

Your thoughts

39
Judgement
(The Prophets, Jesus, Revelation)

Our world reeks with injustice. Tyrants torture and kill. The environment withers under our abuse. Greed dominates the landscape. If ever humanity risked the judgement of God, it is now.

Yet our contemporary world has no fear of such judgement. We hear no warning salvos from the pulpits of the mainline churches. In thirty years of preaching, I don't remember ever having focused a sermon on God's judgement! We — and I include myself — do not tremble in dread of divine retribution. The notion that western society, largely the product of Christianity, stands under the judgement of God and is in danger of being destroyed, is a foreign concept to most of us.

But that is precisely the point I want to make.

A quick delve into the Bible reveals judgement as a common theme. The prophets were especially good at warning of the imminent judgement of God, and at least some people greatly feared it.

Things are different today. Whatever God we believe in, or don't believe in, does not leave us standing in awe and fear. We know that the thunder and lightning is not God out to get us. We can't even imagine how God might bring judgement. Warnings about the next world carry little weight since our concern is with this one!

(I need to be careful with blanket statements. For many, judgement is very real. Fanned on by the fundamentalists, they take God's judgement very seriously. I, however, do not speak for these people, but to the searchers and seekers who have lost, if they ever had, any sense of living under the judgement of God.)

Love as judgement

The mainline liberal Protestant images God as a very sentimental God of love who would not dream of doing us any harm. And yes, I affirm that God is love. But this does not mean that there is no judgement.

We forget about "tough love." It is precisely because God is love that we stand under judgement.

We know the judgement of love in the normal course of our everyday lives. Judgement comes in the form of corrupted and unfulfilling relationships with self, others, the earth, and God. To fail to yearn for and work for my marriage partner's fullness of life, with the same passion I expend on myself (and who achieves that?), will result in an incomplete relationship. The same goes for every relationship. I can manage it only when I am fully in possession of myself and whole, and when is that?

Nothing tests the quality of my character as love does.

In fact, love is the ultimate arbiter in every aspect of my life. Love is a law. It operates everywhere. Love, then, is the law in the workplace, the corporation, the government, the family, everywhere. If we violate it, bad things will happen.

This is simply another way of saying that our immaturity, or lack of wholeness, our blindness, our insensitivity, causes all the problems of humanity. In an erotic universe that seeks to be an embodiment of love, the failure to love will always have dire consequences.

Ultimately, every violation of love is a sin against Eros, a misuse of the universal creative, yearning, energy. Eros is not a distant God but one who surrounds and permeates us as the elemental force behind, through, around, and in everything. There is no escape, no place to hide.

The Psalmist prayed, "Against you, you alone, have I sinned." (Psalm 51:4a) Traditionally, this Psalm is attributed to David after Nathan confronted him for his adultery with Bethsheba. She could be forgiven for thinking that the sin was against her rather than God. But any particular sin is also a crime against the nature of the universe, Eros, God.

Judgement in the unfolding of history

The prophets saw the judgement of God in the unfolding of history, and especially in the disasters that befell the Hebrew people. They were right. They uttered judgements against all the nations, for they saw that justice and love are required in all places. But they especially focused on Israel and Judah. Amos thundered, "Hear this word that the Lord has spoken against you, O people of Israel, against the whole family that I brought up out of the land of Egypt: You only have I known of all the families of the earth; therefore I will punish you for all your iniquities."(Amos 3:1-2)

Judgement is not the arbitrary act of an angry God sitting on a distant throne, but is written into the fabric of history.

We reap what we sow, although I use "we" in a very general sense. The people who sow are usually not the ones who reap. The world abounds with innocent victims. Our personal sins may well come back to haunt us, but often others suffer worse than we do. The victims of injustice and discrimination suffer because of the social system and not because of personal wrongdoing.

Eros will be vindicated

Eros will be vindicated. Life cannot be ultimately squelched. Liberation theology tells us that God has a preferential option for the poor, and for all victims of oppression. Stirrings for justice will come from the place of most acute pain. When my yearning for life is thwarted, it will burn in me. If I can, I will do something about it. If not, and it may take generations, a community of discontent will build until it cannot be denied.

Whenever the leaders in religion, government, business, communities, or families, or any one of us, act from any motivation other than the good of the earth and her people, the flow of history will ultimately bring judgement.

The elemental force of life is at work. Life — Eros/God — will always push toward a just and caring society. Dictators need to tremble before the yearning of their people, for this is God at work. It is Eros doing what Eros does. Ultimately, there is no escape.

Nor is western society immune. How long can our world sustain, or the people of the world put up with, our excesses? Eros, as the yearning of history, will bring our unsustainable society to an end. In fact, it is now happening. We hope that the process is evolution rather than revolution. However it comes about, we know judgement is inevitable.

It is the judgement of God.

Reflection questions

1. Do you feel judged by parents, society, God, yourself? And, if so, how does this feeling influence your life?
2. How can we talk of judgement with the countless innocent victims of history?
3. How are we violating the law of love as individuals and as a society?

Your thoughts

40
The quality of Jesus' life
(Jesus' life)

What songs did Mary sing to Jesus? What stories did Joseph tell him? Did his father die early? (we hear of Joseph only in the birth and the temple-at-twelve accounts.) Can we find anything in Jesus' background or upbringing which explains, or even helps explain, the quality of his person?

The church framed the question in a negative way. It talked about the sinlessness of Jesus — which raised the question, "How come he was without sin?" Believing that sin was passed on from parent to child, the virgin birth myth solved half the problem by doing away with one parent. But what about Mary? To make her pure, the idea of the immaculate conception evolved. Such stories have powerful mythic implications, but, as actual history, they carry no weight and undermine Jesus' humanity.

The call of the soul

We look to childhood influences. No doubt our childhood is one facet in the mix that makes us, but perhaps not the most important. James Hillman, in *The Soul's Code,* has a chapter on "The Parental Fallacy."[1]

Hillman maintains that we are shaped by the inner call of the soul. As a start, the soul chooses the genes that will incarnate it; thus we choose our parents! When I first heard this theory, it sounded to me like some strange new-age idea. Hillman is, however, a highly-regarded Jungian analyst worthy of our attention. His insight affirms the involvement of the mythic realm in the soul making process, which I have discussed earlier.

The truth must lie somewhere in the mix of genes and soul.

In thinking upon the source of the high quality of Jesus' character, I lean toward Hillman. Jesus became who he was primarily because the Self, the collective unconscious, had chosen him for the task. Jesus consciously took on the messiah role at his baptism, but the messiah energy or archetype had been working in him long before. As Hillman suggests, who we are intended to be works in us from the moment of our birth, and perhaps long before.

After we are born the soul must do what it can to create the person appropriate to the self seeking incarnation. To do this, the soul can use every experience of life to nudge us toward our calling. Perhaps some situation calls out for justice, and something within us responds. Perhaps we are stirred by music or art, and are called in that direction. Perhaps a hard childhood made us sensitive to child abuse and we feel impelled to work in that area.

Anything can help us know ourselves. This is a comforting thought. It means that our strengths and weaknesses, successes and failures, the negative as well as the positive aspects of our childhood, all have a role in creating us. We must exorcize the demons in our lives, but the question we need to ask is, "What did that experience teach us about ourselves and life?" To use a favourite phrase of Jean Houston, "You must do your therapy, but your therapy won't do it for you." You must also listen to the call of the soul.

The real trick is developing the necessary self-possession, or ego strength, to carry the self growing within us. This means having the inner strength to come to terms with our childhood and all the experiences of life. Only a clear-eyed acceptance of our historical reality can let us get on with growing more and more into our true selves.

Integrity as self-possession

Whatever therapy Jesus needed, he obviously accomplished without benefit of modern psychology.

What he said and did came out of a profound sureness and self-possession that amazed those who met him. "Never has anyone spoken like this!" (John 7:46) "They were astonished at his teaching, for he taught them as one having authority, and not as the scribes." (Mark 1:22) For Jesus to say, "You have heard that it was said to those of ancient times . . . . but I say to you. . ." (Matthew 5:21-22) required an inner knowing that most of us can, at best, only glimpse.

Jesus possessed an awesome integrity. He had himself together. He was of one piece. His words and his actions were "in sync." In this sense, the church rightly thought of him as sinless.

Integrity requires inner strength. Jesus had it. He was not overwhelmed by the challenges that faced him. He had to work out the answers, but he looked at them, met them, and solved them rather than allowing them to weaken or destroy him. He was a problem-solver rather than a self-doubter. He wasted no time and energy struggling with supposed inadequacies.

Integrity as humility

Integrity also requires humility. I define humility as knowing who you are and knowing you are not God.

That raises interesting questions in relation to Jesus, whom the later church did see as God. He didn't see himself in that light. Even though he was the Messiah, in his humanness he had to attune to and be the servant of his calling, that is, of God. Again and again the synoptic gospels tell us of Jesus going off by himself to pray. He needed times of aloneness with the great Mystery that sought to become real in the world through him. Jesus had the humility to know himself to be the servant of the purpose of God.

John's gospel, a profound reflection on Jesus' life, saw both Jesus' oneness with and separateness from God: a true humility. The writer has Jesus say, "The father is greater than I" (John 14:28b), clearly establishing difference and separateness. The writer, however, also affirms their oneness by having Jesus say, "Believe me that I am in the Father and the Father is in me" (John 14:11), and "The Father and I are one." (John 10:30)

The defining quality

Let integrity stand as the defining quality of Jesus' life.

We cannot know whether Jesus was absolutely "perfect" or "sinless." We do know that the messiah role called him to a profound integrity that was the driving force of his life. It brought him to the Jordan to be baptized, drove him into the wilderness to sort out his calling, sent him on to teach and heal and to face with courage and compassion all he met, and finally to accept his death.

We also know that the quality of his life transformed people, founded a religion, and created a mythology and theology that still has power to heal and make whole.

May the same integrity work in us and enable us to offer our full selves to heal and celebrate the world

Reflection questions

1. Do you feel you were born for some special task or purpose?
Is there a theme that unites the various aspects of your life?
2. What do you believe to be the qualities of an ideal person? Is there a one basic quality?
3. In what ways does a lack of integrity undermine our society?

Your thoughts

41
Jesus' humanity
(The Gospels; Hebrews)

How many ways can I say it? It is the humanity of Jesus that matters. Everything ever said or believed about Jesus is completely, utterly, fully, absolutely, dependent upon the quality of his humanity.

Jesus, the person

The impact of Jesus as a person was the starting point of everything Christian. His first followers met a person. They were unencumbered by the generations of doctrine which grew up around him. They didn't know they were supposed to believe he was Christ or God or anything else. It was the quality of Jesus' person that astounded them. "Never has anyone spoken like this!" (John 7:46)

The disciples left everything to follow him. They did so not because they believed they were following God, or even a Messiah. They simply met a person, but a person of such quality, such inner self-possession, such unflaunted sureness, that they did whatever it took to follow him.

In him they met the fullness of humanity. In him, they found a wholeness and completeness that he not only talked about but lived. He practised what he preached. In him, they saw love in action, and it evoked in them the destiny of their own humanity.

Quite naturally, Jesus' followers used all the words and ideas that came to mind to try to explain and understand him. He was Lord, the great teacher, the wise one. He was the Messiah, the eagerly-awaited deliverer. All sorts of titles and mythologies arose to explain the greatness of the person they met.

The ultimate accolade

Such a great one must certainly have a special relationship with God, but calling Jesus God was a long step for the strictly monotheistic Jews. They believed that there was only one God, and naming Jesus God was adding another. It was the ultimate accolade for

Jesus, but an affront to traditional Jewish faith. Some made the plunge. Perhaps they were nudged on by the Greeks, who had no such difficulty. In the Greek tradition, gods and people did intermingle; being part god and part human was not uncommon.

Ultimately, the church felt that they could only adequately explain the greatness of Jesus by naming him God, one person of the divine trinity of Father, Son, and Holy Spirit.

However, calling Jesus God shifts the emphasis away from the human person.

Which happened. Some thought that Jesus could not have been really human and only appeared so.

I must give orthodoxy its due. The creeds, the official statements of the faith of the church, carefully protected Jesus' humanity. They explained Jesus as being perfectly human and perfectly divine, both at the same time and without compromising either his divinity or humanity. Whether that sounds irrational or not depends upon your vision of God! However we see it, we must acknowledge that from this belief evolved the magnificent edifice of Christian theology, which, over the generations, has nourished countless believers and converted unbelievers.

I fear that we today have lost the clarity of the creeds. Understanding Jesus as divine and human seems contradictory and confusing, so we have turned Jesus into a mixture, with more emphasis on his divinity than his humanity. Many become terribly upset when Jesus' divinity is questioned, but they don't seem to have the same concern about maintaining the purity of his humanity.

We must hold firmly to the awareness that giving Jesus divine status was a way of talking about the quality of his humanity. His humanity came first. Every title, every enlarged story, every mythology resulted from the impact of his humanity.

Hold on to his humanity

In our time, I think it vitally important to hold on to Jesus' humanity. We know something of what being human means, but our concepts of God are often foggy, and not always relevant to our daily life.

If we want to talk about Jesus as divine, we must be clear that his divinity is not something added on to his humanity. If Jesus was more than human, then he was not human. We can't have it both ways.

We must also be clear that if Jesus was more than human, he is useless to us. If he was something I cannot be because I am human, then what's the point? I am relieved of the responsibility of living the quality of humanity that Jesus lived.

Even in Yahweh's view, if I may be so bold, Jesus had to be human. Yahweh, the God image of the Hebrew people, can grow to be the fullness of God only by experiencing being human. That means that the Messiah, the one who is to bear the God archetype, must do so as a human. If Jesus were less than human, or more than human, he would be as useless to Yahweh as to us.

In other words, Jesus' mandate was to live out the messiah archetype, embody Eros in the world, as a human being, "who in every respect has been tested as we are." (Hebrews 4:15b)

Passing on the torch

By being human, Jesus confronts us with the possibility and necessity of being fully human. Jesus says to us, "Look at me! What I am, you can be." He is the hero, the model, the archetype, the mentor, who tells us that we can and must live in the world with the same qualities he possessed. The goal is for "all of us [individually and collectively] [to] come . . . to maturity, to the measure of the full stature of Christ." (Ephesians 4:13)

The writer of John's gospel has Jesus respond to a question by saying, "The one who believes in me will also do the works that I do and, in fact, will do greater works than these." (John 14:12) Obviously he assumed that we are capable of doing such works.

In that case, "Let us run with perseverance the race that is set before us, looking to Jesus the pioneer and perfecter of our faith." (Hebrews 12:1b-2a)

Reflection questions

1. How has your childhood image of Jesus changed over the

years?

2. Does focusing on Jesus' humanity help you, in Marcus Borg's words, to "meet Jesus again for the first time"?

3. In what ways does the quality of Jesus' humanity encourage you to make the best possible use of your life?

Your thoughts

42
The specialness of Jesus
(John; Ephesians)

John's gospel has it right. To understand the specialness of Jesus, we have to go right back to the impulse that first created the universe. John's words, "In the beginning was the Word" (John 1:1), takes us back to the first act of creation and roots Jesus in this cosmic unfolding.

This fact does not of itself make Jesus any different from the rest of us. We have all come out of the creative energy which caused the universe to happen. Each one of us carries in the atoms of our body the history of the universe. For me, that's an awesome thought. Jesus, like the rest of us, has a long history.

John (the writer was very likely named John, but was probably not John the disciple) calls this creative force "the Word," a concept we have met before. The Bible uses Word (Logos) and Wisdom (Sophia) to indicate that one aspect of the nature of the Ultimate Mystery is creativity. Wisdom says, "When [God] marked out the foundations of the earth, then I was beside him, like a master worker." (Proverbs 8:29-30) John echoes Proverbs' description of Sophia in describing the Word: "All things came into being through [the Word], and without him not one thing came into being." (John 1:3)

We have looked at these things before. I now want to emphasize that humanity, including Jesus, comes from the same creative energy that caused the universe. God, the restless Eros energy that yearns for companionship with a creature of like nature, finally evolved humanity.

Let me review the long road to becoming human.

Creating humanity turned out to be a long and arduous task, and is still in progress. This human creature, in order to be capable of full and complete communion with the creator, has to be independent, conscious, aware, mature, complete. As in any marriage, the partners must come to one another as free, independent persons. When God and humanity are the partners, this is not easily achieved.

Maturity is not something that we can be given. We must earn it and learn it.

The process started with the Big Bang. In the evolving universe, whose purpose as far as we can tell is to companion the creator, there eventually appeared a creature capable of consciousness. This giant step into conscious awareness is mythically expressed by Eve eating the forbidden fruit. She, with the help of the snake, developed enough self-awareness to defy God and eat the forbidden fruit. By disobeying, she demonstrated the independent will necessary for growth.

Eve is each of us at our "terrible two" stage. The independent step has been taken, but there is a long way to go. The biblical story tells us of the struggle of a people to complete what Eve started.

The Hebrews grow in inner strength

It takes a long time, and few ever achieve it, to develop the inner strength necessary to incarnate our full purpose in the world. It took the Hebrew people the entire period of what we call the Old Testament before a person could have that level of self-possession.

Job is a crucial turning point. He had the maturity to realize his own righteousness and not be intimidated by Yahweh. It does not matter if Job is a story rather than an account of actual events. It happened in the psyche of the writer and was thus implanted in the Hebrew experience.

An experience or insight does not just sit there. It activates an archetypal energy that continues to work in the collective psyche of the people. Job, clinging to his integrity in the face of an abusive Yahweh, demonstrated a giant step in developing the energy of wholeness that Eve had set in motion.

This energy, strengthened by Job, would not be satisfied until one appeared who would carry the fullness of the purpose of humanity, one truly created in the image of God. Yahweh needed to incarnate as a human person.

Yearning for the Messiah

In the centuries before Jesus' birth, a yearning grew among the Hebrew people for a Messiah to appear. In the decades and years before his birth, this desire reached fever pitch. The activated archetype was growing stronger and stronger.

For the most part, they envisaged the Messiah as a political leader who would free them from Roman rule. A few had deeper insight and understood the Messiah as one who would fulfil their purpose in history.

Who and what such a person would be could be known only after the fact. Jesus had to live out his life as the Messiah, as one who carried the fullness of the divine image in human form, before we could know what being human really involves.

The Word made flesh

John summarizes all this in one short sentence: "And the Word became flesh and lived among us." (John 1:14) The Mystery where selves are born gave Jesus the task of incarnating, or living out in history, the essence of human life — to live as the human presence of Eros, the love of God incarnate.

In this, Jesus is different from us. I believe we are all given gifts and have a unique role to play in the unfolding human drama, but we are not called to be the Messiah. That role belonged to Jesus.

Ultimately we must all be incarnations of love. But it cannot happen "until all of us . . . come to maturity, to the measure of the full stature of Christ." (Ephesians 4:13)

This is a communal effort. In the Christian scheme, Jesus plays a pivotal role, but each of us has a place and a responsibility. The passage in Ephesians to which I have referred several times describes the process. After Jesus had lived out the nature of divinity, the archetype of wholeness was greatly focused and strengthened. "When he ascended on high . . . he gave gifts to his people . . . . to equip [them] for . . . building up the body of Christ [humanity], until all of us come to . . . maturity . . . Speaking the truth in love, we must grow up in every way into him who is the head, into

Christ. . . . [When] each part is working properly, [it] promotes the body's growth in building itself up in love." (Ephesians 4:8-16)

Jesus, as the Christ, became a beacon who has gone before us. Within his light we are called, not to be Christ, but to be one of the "properly working" parts of the body. In this way, we do our part in helping all humanity grow to the fullness of Christ's maturity.

Reflection questions

1. Take some meditative time and imagine the atoms that make up your body evolving from the moment of the Big Bang until they formed you. What are your thoughts and feelings?
2. Continuing in meditative mode, think about particular people of the past or present who have special meaning for you as part of the process of humanity growing toward wholeness. Who are they and what role did they play?
3. Where do you see yourself in the grand drama? What is your specialness?

Your thoughts

43
Was Jesus God?
(John; Philippians; Colossians; Revelation)

The creeds have always affirmed that Jesus is both God and human, without one compromising the other. Being God did not compromise his humanity, nor did being human lessen his being God. For most people that was too big a thought to grasp, so they tended to see Jesus as a supernatural person who could do what it was believed God could do.

With the disappearance of God from our modern world, the whole notion of Jesus as God-man made no sense. The concept lost its relevance for our modern, western, scientific, this-world only, mindset.

Unfortunately, the church often lags behind in taking account of these changes. The 'Jesus' question became a public issue in The United Church of Canada only a few years ago when the then Moderator, the Very Rev. Bill Phipps, in an interview with the *Ottawa Citizen*, volunteered that he did not believe in virgin births or physical resurrections, or that Jesus was the whole of God.

The Moderator's comments, while offending some, helped the church to catch up with the way the western world thinks. We need to recognize that just because an idea was alive in past ages does not mean it is alive today. Our modern scientific, secular, rationalistic way of thinking would be totally foreign to people a few centuries ago.

What we believe about Jesus has been caught in this swing. The church continues to proclaim dogmas formulated centuries ago to a world, and to the world within every Christian, that now has no way of understanding what is being said. The church has kept talking about Jesus as God without realizing that the whole discussion has become largely irrelevant, because we are clear about neither the Jesus we meet in the gospels nor what we understand by the term "God."

"God," in fact, has been the chief casualty of our modern world. Our modern way of thinking leaves little room for God. As

Bonhoeffer said years ago, "what we call 'God' is being more and more edged out of life, losing more and more ground."[2] We thought we had the mystery captured within the doctrine of the church, but we didn't. God escaped. If you want to delve into a really thorough discussion, read Karen Armstrong's *A Brief History of God*, Mary Jean Irion's *From the Ashes of Christianity*, or Bishop John Shelby Spong's, *Why Christianity Must Change or Die*.

The real question

The real question about Jesus is not whether he is God but what he can offer a world searching for meaning and even survival.

In fact, Jesus remains an intriguing and compelling figure both within and far beyond the borders of the church. The Jesus Seminar makes secular headlines. Bookstores have shelves of books on Jesus. Add the fuss caused by the United Church Moderator's plain talk, Bishop John Shelby Spong's controversial books, the religious websites, innumerable study groups, and it's apparent that Jesus interests many people.

We now have a new search for Jesus as a person within the context of his time.

We now recognize that it was his impact as a person that caused all the stir. Describing Jesus as God was a way of stressing the importance of Jesus for peoples' lives. Jesus' followers found in him the clue that made sense of their lives and gave them both a personal and cosmic meaning. They struggled to find ways of saying that Jesus was for them the mirror of their own souls and a window on the heart of the universe, that is, on God. We need not be surprised that they described Jesus as divine.

The Bible says

Scholars argue over whether or not the New Testament writers give Jesus the status of God. They certainly saw Jesus as divine, although they never attempted to sort out what that meant within a strict monotheism.

The eloquent opening of John's gospel leaves no doubt that the writer intended to put Jesus right up there with God. "In the beginning was the Word, and the Word was with God, and the

Word was God . . . . And the Word became flesh and lived among us." (John 1:1,14)

Even before the gospels were written, an early hymn of the church, quoted by Paul in his letter to the Philippians, sees Jesus "in the form of God." (Philippians 2:6a)

The writer of Colossians saw Jesus in a cosmic context. "He is the image of the invisible God . . . . and in him all things hold together . . . . For in him all the fullness of God was pleased to dwell." (Colossians 1:15-19)

The book of Revelation constantly speaks of God (the one seated on the throne) and Jesus (the Lamb) in the same breath. (e.g., Revelation 5:13)

Jesus as God becomes orthodox

Later, councils of church leaders would argue over whether Jesus was of "the same substance" as "the Father," or only of "like substance." The "same substance" folks won. That meant that the "orthodox" position understood Jesus as part of the Godhead within the rather confusing doctrine of the trinity.

The church has tended to equate "orthodox" with "truth" — a dangerous mistake. At one level, orthodoxy is simply the theological position that could muster the most votes at the various church councils. At another level, it represents the amount of truth the church could cope with at that particular time. Tragically, though, the church's thinking often stays locked into the thought forms of the age in which these pronouncements were made.

Questioning is not new

Doubters and questioners have kept the church alive and in tune with the world. In fact, theology is the constant attempt to find the words to make the faith real and alive for the present day. It is an endless task and one I'm happy to be involved in.

Our present discussions regarding Jesus carry on this theological work. When we simply repeat past formulations of theology, we risk locking the power of the person of Jesus within the dogma of his being God. As Marcus J. Borg, of the Jesus Seminar, titled his book, we are now *Meeting Jesus Again for the First Time*.

We need to find ways of talking about the specialness of Jesus, but no particular words will ever be adequate.

I do have a couple of "bottom lines," though, which any discussion of Jesus must honour.

First, any definition which compromises Jesus' humanity is unacceptable.

Secondly, we must have humility in relation to other religions. We have often assumed that having Jesus as God makes our religion superior. That assumption is no longer acceptable. If humanity is to survive, we need all the help available from all sources. We must offer our truth, but we must listen to others knowing that we and the world need their truth as well.

Whatever we say about him, Jesus rings down through the ages with the transforming power of one who confronts us with the possibilities and inadequacies of ourselves and our world. If that fits into your concept of God, that's fine.

✧ ✧ ✧

Reflection questions

1. Has the "death of God" been real for you? If so, what has it meant for your spiritual journey?
2. How do you see Jesus as a help in facing the monstrous evils rampant in our world?
3. How have your doubts nourished your faith?

Your thoughts

44
Jesus Died For Me?
(The passion narratives in the gospels)

Jesus' death fascinates Christians.

If you have any Christian connection, you will have heard many clichés about being saved by the blood of the lamb, being washed in the blood, Jesus dying for our sins, dying to save us from sin, dying to assure us that we will go to heaven, and such things. The words of an old hymn summarize the church's traditional thinking: "He died that we might be forgiven, He died to make us good, That we might go at last to heaven, Saved by his precious blood."

I find the images offensive and the theology outdated, but Jesus' death still touches some deep inner cord.

A long tradition

This interest goes right back to the New Testament. An account of Jesus' passion (the events surrounding his death) forms the dramatic climax of each of the four New Testament gospels. Paul's whole theology is founded upon the death and resurrection of Jesus: "While we still were sinners Christ died for us." (Romans 5:8) The letter to the Hebrews focuses on the image of sacrifice, saying that Christ "offered for all time a single sacrifice for sins." (Hebrews 10:12) John's gospel uses the sacrificial lamb image, which is also central to the book of Revelation: "Worthy is the Lamb that was slaughtered." (Revelation 5:12)

The church's primary ritual, the Eucharist, uses bread and wine as symbols of Jesus' body broken and blood shed. The central symbol of the church is the cross and, for much of the church, the crucifix (Jesus hanging on the cross).

Our history, our traditions, our rituals, all point relentlessly to Jesus' death.

There is something elemental about Jesus' death, something that penetrates to the very heart of life. We find ourselves more deeply involved than as mere onlookers or voyeurs at a gruesome execution. We know we are somehow involved. We feel Jesus' death resonate with the depths of our nature.

Jesus, the innocent victim

That Jesus died as an innocent victim shakes us. That he died prematurely and without personal guilt at the hands of the religious and political authorities and with the clamouring of the crowd jars our sense of justice.

We find it harder to understand how we could possibly be at fault. We did not, after all, personally put Jesus to death. Yet the old black spiritual poses the question that haunts us, "Were you there when they crucified my Lord?"

Over the centuries, the darker side of the church has avoided the issue by indulging in the age-old blaming game and accusing the Jews of killing Jesus. Jews and Romans, of course, actually did the deed. We need to know, and need to keep reminding ourselves, that they were no more evil than the rest of us. In the same situation, any group of people, including ourselves, could well have done the same thing.

When we meet with more light, more truth, more of the reality of ourselves than we can cope with, we tend to "shoot the messenger." Very stupid things happen. Socrates had to drink the hemlock. Galileo had to deny his knowledge that the earth moves around the sun. We beat up our partners. We go to war. How many times has someone been ostracized, fired, or otherwise victimized for exposing wrongdoing? Jesus, a victim of human maliciousness and folly, was crucified.

No, we did not personally kill Jesus. But his death sits there judging our hypocrisy and exclusions, our dividing of the world into "us" and "them," our self-righteous condemnation of others.

Failed integrity

All those connected with Jesus' death, both individuals and institutions, failed to live up to their own integrity. The political leaders failed to carry out justice, the religious leaders closed their minds to new truth, the disciples lost their nerve, and the people succumbed to crowd hysteria.

We are made of no different stuff than those people. We, too, have a dark side, and in certain situations know not how we might respond. Being human means bearing the burden of the dark side of history.

We cannot escape by turning to our institutions. The shining integrity of Jesus would blow apart any present day religious or political system. In the political arena, power corrupts, and every organization or grouping of people is political. The thought that "we are right" blinkers any religious group or belief system. (I, of course, am exempt!) Giving our ultimate allegiance to any institution, even a religious one, is demonic.

We are still, as Paul put it, "in Adam" — "Adam" being the symbol of immature humanity. (Paul, patriarchal to the end, fails to acknowledge Eve's role.) In biblical terms, we are all sinners, separated from our wholeness.

Creative and destructive urges battle within us. We have made enormous strides, but how much energy have we wasted in building and using both internal and external defences? War has dominated the human story. Psychology has revealed to us that our internal complexes and defence mechanisms are equally, or more, complex than our external protective systems.

Something deep stirred

Jesus' death stirs and confronts us. By experiencing physically, psychically, and spiritually, the full impact of our demonic side, Jesus leaves us exposed and defenceless. We know that, in the same situation, we could be found wanting. Because he held onto his integrity "and became obedient to the point of death" (Philippians 2:8), we feel a powerful call to our own integrity and the integrity of the world around us.

Paul sums it up by saying, "As all die in Adam, so all will be made alive in Christ." (I Corinthians 15:22) "In Christ" means we are called to live the truth of our own lives and to call the world (governments, corporations, religions, individuals) to integrity and wholeness.

In this imperfect world, we will pay a price for our integrity — but not, we hope, as high a price as Jesus paid. We will also experience fulfilment and joy. Jesus, "for the sake of the joy that was set before him endured the cross . . . and has taken his seat at the right hand of the throne of God." (Hebrews 12:2)

Yes, Jesus died for us. Yes, Jesus' death opens for us a door to life. From his vantage point beside the throne he promises us encouragement and help.

Reflection questions

1. Do you see more in our interest in Jesus' death than a morbid fascination with violence and death?
2. The suffering of the innocent exposes the guilt of those who carry out the world's evil. What situations evoke your anger and your passion for justice?
3. Are there ways in which Jesus, as a classic example of the innocent victim, exposes your complicity in the world's evil and your need to deal with your own lack of wholeness?

Your thoughts

45
The route to joy
(Matthew 26:26-29; Mark 14:22-25; Luke 22:15-20; 1 Cor. 11:23-26)

The Eucharist, Holy Communion, the Lord's Supper, the Mass — whatever we call the ritual meal Jesus shared with his disciples "on the night when he was betrayed" (1 Corinthians 11:23b) — has always been the most holy act of Christian worship.

And rightly so. It is the ritual act that incorporates us into the essence of the Christian faith: the life, death, and resurrection of Jesus the Christ. As such, it should be the most joyous of celebrations. For me, and I suspect for many, experiencing that gladness within the Eucharist has taken some time.

Childhood experience

I have always known that Communion is the most holy of holy acts. I should. I grew up in Pictou County, Nova Scotia, the heartland of Presbyterianism, where religion, and especially Communion, was taken very seriously.

Certainly in Scotsburn, my home church, Communion was a serious and solemn business. In my youth, there were still echoes of the great Communion seasons of generations before, although I don't remember the use of tokens (having a token indicated you were fit to take Communion). We did have Preparatory Service on Friday evening to purify us for the great occasion to come on Sunday.

In my earliest years, the children had to leave when Communion time came. After a few years, however, we were allowed to stay but were warned to be absolutely quiet and still and, of course, we were not allowed to partake of the bread and wine. I remember it as an awesome time. The elders sat up front looking very stern. The minister went through some mumbo jumbo that sounded very holy. The elders distributed the bread and then the grape juice; real wine was beyond the pale. One of the elders had squeaky shoes, but I dared not laugh.

The awesomeness and holiness of the occasion certainly imprinted itself upon my young psyche. Joy, however, is not a word that springs to mind to describe it.

Communion seemed like a solemn remembrance of a very sad occasion, Jesus' death. It certainly brought us "face to face" with the reality that he had died. What connection Communion had with my life remained unclear.

Even in my adult life as a minister, privileged to conduct communion, the joyous dimension of this holy act developed slowly.

Communion was, however, always a high point of my ministry. To break the bread and say, "Jesus said, 'This is my body, broken for you'," and to lift the cup and say, "This is my blood, shed for you," was always an ecstatic moment. Something profound was happening that I could only dimly know. To fully experience the joyous message of Communion, though, I still had a long way to go.

Then one evening a few years ago, I was receiving Communion as one of the worshippers at Kim McAuley's covenanting service. Suddenly, joy welled through me. I could feel the energy spread from some centre point through my whole body. My hair and toes tingled. Something in me said, "Yes, I am celebrating the route to joy."

Through death to life

The writer to the Hebrews had it right when she (one scholarly opinion, not widely accepted, believes that a woman wrote this biblical letter) said of Jesus, "who for the sake of the joy that was set before him endured the cross." (Hebrews 12:2) Paying the price and the joy of fulfilment are connected.

Jesus introduced this sacred meal as he and his disciples celebrated the Passover, the central ritual meal of the Jewish faith. Tension filled the air. He had come to Jerusalem at Passover time and by his "triumphal entry" and "cleansing the temple" had raised the ire of both the political and religious authorities. Now his death was imminent. To give his disciples a ritual by which to remember him, he put a new twist on the Passover meal. Instead of the lamb being the sacrificed animal, he held up the bread and wine symbolizing that he was the sacrifice. He himself was the lamb.

In that moment at Kim's covenanting service, I knew at a new level that I was being drawn into the integrity, compassion, courage, and faithfulness that marked Jesus' life and for which he died. Sharing in the ritual empowered me, in some degree, to live my life with the same tenacious integrity and courage that Jesus embodied. The result was joy.

I learned that the ultimate joy and fulfilment of life comes through hanging tough as we do what we can or must do in bringing wholeness to ourselves and the world.

Resurrection

We call the new life we experience resurrection. We know it when we have intentionally carried through on a hard path that life has required of us.

Celebrating Communion moves us beyond Jesus' life and death to participate in his resurrection. Our grief at his death, our sorrow for the darkness within us and our world, breaks through to the joy of resurrection. We experience resurrection in the here and now, but we are also drawn into the cosmic drama which Jesus precipitated when he took "his seat at the right hand of the throne of God." (Hebrews 12:2b) This theme is further developed in the book of Revelation.

We eat this bread and drink this cup to be strengthened by Jesus' life, death, and resurrection. Empowered to go out into the world with the truth of our lives, we will know joy, just as Jesus, "for the sake of the joy that was set before him endured the cross." (Hebrews 12:2)

Reflection questions

1. Can you (especially if you are not involved with the institutional church) use the Eucharist as a model to help you develop rituals which enable you to embody human qualities?
2. What brings you joy?
3. As this book draws to a close, review the stages in your own inner journey and what you have offered to the world for healing and the celebration of life.

46
Yahweh becomes whole
(Revelation)

Time now to conclude our imaginative sojourn with the growing Yahweh.

Yahweh, following Jesus' death, must have been a confused and sorrowful wreck. Incarnation within a human life would bring an ultimate cosmic joy. In Jesus, Yahweh had tasted this supreme fulfilment. But now, Yahweh was left bereft and grief-stricken, having helplessly stood by as Jesus died.

Yahweh experienced, there on the cross, both death and the death of a beloved one. Perhaps we catch a glimpse of the Yahweh experience when one member of an intimately loving couple of many years dies. Something of the person left both dies and knows the death of the beloved. We can feel a deep compassion for Yahweh.

In the process, Yahweh would develop a new level of passion and compassion for humanity. Having tasted the rich fare of incarnation, Yahweh could never again be satisfied with existence in only the mythic realm. Nor could Yahweh become a true image of the ultimate divine Eros without a deep communion with the human.

Yahweh badly needed healing. Guilt hangs heavy. Yahweh as a patriarchal male God- image was complicit in Jesus' death. The energy that had been arrogant, intimidating, and insensitive proved demonic. Yahweh's own shadow side was now exposed. In Jesus, Yahweh had tasted wholeness and must now become whole. Yahweh's compassion, which had always been present but not always visible, must now rule.

The book of Revelation

We witness this healing process in the Book of Revelation, a grand mythic vision of the events initiated, both in heaven and on earth, by the return to heaven of the Messiah archetype. It is a great story worthy of a whole book — which is to say I hope to write one some day!

In the middle of the book we have a picture of the healing of Yahweh. It happens in the form of a battle in heaven. "And war broke out in heaven; Michael and his angels fought against the dragon. The dragon and his angels fought back, but they were defeated, and there was no longer any place for them in heaven." (Revelation 12:7-8) The energy within Yahweh that had turned demonic, here called "the dragon," was exorcized. Yahweh is now whole. The fullness of Eros now lives in Yahweh.

Yet Yahweh cannot fully enjoy wholeness until humanity also becomes whole. Yahweh must have a mature and fully-aware partner. What Yahweh experienced in Jesus was now part of the package. Yahweh's final fulfilment could come only with a union with the whole of humanity – and that is, in essence, the story of the book of Revelation.

The final human struggle begins when "the great dragon was thrown down . . . to the earth." (Revelation 12:9) The demonic energy that lived in the mythic realm is now released upon the earth. The battle in heaven now becomes a battle on earth. The dragon (Yahweh's demonic, shadow side) must now be exorcized and transformed in the human realm. But when facing extinction, demonic forces will fight with a vicious ferocity.

This Armageddon struggle, envisioned in the book of Revelation, is a truly mythic account. We should not read it as a literal account of what has happened, or what will happen. Rather, it forms a metaphor for patterns and events in human history and for what must occur before the human family comes to maturity and the final great consummation is achieved.

The visions are often violent and bloody, but, ultimately, the book of Revelation brings profound hope. The final vision pictures complete oneness. The human, the mythic, and the cosmic come together. Heaven and earth unite in a final orgasmic moment where all desire ceases in unity of being. Only then will the elemental yearning of both ourselves and the universe be satisfied.

The New Jerusalem

The New Jerusalem is the biblical image for this final union. The writer of Revelation pictures it this way: "Then I saw a new heaven and a new earth; for the first heaven and the first earth had passed away, and the sea was no more. And I saw the holy city, the new Jerusalem, coming down out of heaven from God, prepared as a bride adorned for her husband." (Revelation 21:1-2) Heaven and earth are wed.

In this New Jerusalem, there is no need of a temple, "for its temple is the Lord God the Almighty and the Lamb." (Revelation 21:22) Yahweh, the Cosmic Christ (the Lamb), and humanity dwell in the same place. "The river of the water of life" flows "from the throne of God and of the Lamb through the middle of the street of the city." (Revelation 22:1-2a) The water of life flows abundantly and everyone may drink of it.

The vision continues: "On either side of the river, is the tree of life with its twelve kinds of fruit." (Revelation 22:2b) How a tree could be on both sides of the river at once is a bit puzzling, but Revelation is radio and not television! The fruit, defying the usual seasonal pattern, appears monthly, assuring great plenty. "The leaves of the tree are for the healing of the nations" (Revelation 22:2c), assuring us that this is a healing place for the whole human family.

Eve's venture achieved

Eve's bold venture into consciousness has finally achieved its purpose. Both Yahweh and humanity have arrived at full maturity. The fearful, jealous, vindictive Yahweh, who evicted Eve and Adam from the garden, is now the open, loving, compassionate Yahweh who says, "Let everyone who is thirsty come. Let anyone who wishes take the water of life as a gift." (Revelation 22:17b) The river, the trees, and the city are there for all.

This final time of fulfilment exists only in myth. It holds out an inviting vision of hope, of which we catch glimpses every time we know love. The final fulfilment is not yet. The human arena is still too dangerous to fully live love without dire results.

For Jesus, the price was death. For Yahweh, the price was being confronted with the absolute necessity of growing up. For humanity, the struggle against the forces of darkness continues. Individually, it means the cost of living our true lives.

Much is required of us. Humanity must become a community of wholeness. Each of us must grow as we can and offer our gifts and destiny to the building up of the human family. The story is individual, communal, and cosmic, and each of us plays a role in the drama!

May love surround you, may joy gladden you, and may your life, and the lives of all those whom you touch, go well.

Reflection questions

1. Review the sweep of human growth from Eve to the New Jerusalem, including the role played by Yahweh and the mythic, and Eros or the Unitive dimension of reality.
2. What steps do you need to take now?
3. What questions and issues are left to be dealt with?

Your thoughts

Notes

1. James Hillman. *The Soul's Code: In Search of Character and Calling*. (New York: Random House, 1996), ch. 3.
2. Dietrich Bonhoeffer. *Prisoner For God: Letters and Papers from Prison*. (New York: The Macmillan Company, 1954), p. 146.

For further reading

Altizer, Thomas J. J. *The Genesis of God: A Theological Genealogy.* Louisville, Ken.: Westminster/John Knox Press, 1993.

Ancient Wisdom and Modern Science. Ed. Stanislav Grof. Albany, N.Y.: State University of New York Press, 1984.

Armstrong, Karen. *A History of God: The 4,000 - Year Quest of Judaism, Christianity and Islam.* New York: Ballantine Books, 1993.

——. *In the Beginning: A New Interpretation of Genesis.* New York: Ballantine Books, 1996.

Biallas, Leonard J. *Myths: Gods, Heroes, and Saviors.* Mystic, Conn.: Twenty-Third Publications, 1986.

Bolen, Jean Shinoda. *Goddesses in Everywoman: A New Psychology of Women.* New York: Harper & Row, 1984.

——. *Gods In Everyman: A New Psychology of Men's Lives & Loves.* New York: Harper & Row, 1989

Bonhoeffer, Dietrich. *Prisoner for God: Letters and Papers from Prison.* Ed. Eberhard Bethge. Trans. Reginald H. Fuller. New York: The Macmillan Company, 1954.

Borg, Marcus J. *Meeting Jesus Again for the First Time: The Historical Jesus & the Heart of Contemporary Faith.* New York: HarperSanFrancisco, 1994.

——. *The God We Never Knew: Beyond Dogmatic Religion to a More Authentic Contemporary Faith.* New York: HarperSanFrancisco, 1997.

Brueggemann, Walter. *The Creative Word: Canon as a Model for Biblical Education.* Philadelphia, Penn: Fortress Press, 1982.

——. *Hope Within History.* Atlanta, Ga.: John Knox Press, 1987.

——. *Texts Under Negotiation: The Bible and Postmodern Imagination.* Minneapolis, Minn.: Fortress Press, 1993.

Campbell, Joseph. *The Hero With a Thousand Faces* (Bollingen Series XVII). New York: Princeton University Press, 1949.

——. *The Masks of God: Creative Mythology.* New York: The Penguin Group, Viking Penguin Inc, 1968.

——. *The Inner Reaches of Outer Space: Metaphor as Myth and as Religion.* New York: Harper & Row, 1988.

Capra, Fritjof. *The Tao of Physics: A exploration of the parallels between modern physics and Eastern mysticism.* London, Eng.: Fontana Paperbacks, 1986.

Capra, Fritjof, David Steindl-Rast. *Belonging to the Universe: Explorations on the Frontiers of Science and Spirituality.* New York:

HarperSanFrancisco, 1991.

Carmody, Denise Lardner. *Mythological Woman: Contemporary Reflections on Ancient Religious Stories*. New York: The Crossroads Publishing Company, 1992.

Chaisson, Eric. *The Life Era: Cosmic Selection and Conscious Evolution*. New York: W.W. Norton & Company, 1987.

Chopra, Deepak. *The Way of the Wizard: Twenty Spiritual Lessons for Creating the Life You Want*. New York: Harmony Books, 1995.

Crossan, John Dominic. *Jesus: A Revolutionary Biography*. New York: HarperSanFrancisco, 1994.

——. *The Birth of Christianity: Discovering What Happened in the Years Immediately After the Execution of Jesus*. New York: HarperSanFrancisco, 1998.

Davies, Paul. *The Cosmic Blueprint: New Discoveries in Nature's Creative Ability to Order the Universe*. New York: Simon & Schuster, 1988.

——. *About Time: Einstein's Unfinished Revolution*. New York: Simon & Schuster, 1995.

DiCarlo, Russell E. *Towards a New World Order: Conversations at the Leading Edge*. Erie, Penn.: Epic Publishing, 1996.

Dossey, Larry. *Rediscovering the Soul: A Scientific and Spiritual Search*. New York: Bantam Books, 1989.

Dourley, John P. *A Strategy for a Loss of Faith: Jung's Proposal*. Toronto: Inner City Books, 1992.

——. *The Illness That We Are: A Jungian Critique of Christianity*. Toronto: Inner City Books, 1984.

Dwinell, Michael. *Fire Bearer: Evoking a Priestly Humanity*. Liguori, Mo.: Triumph Books, 1993.

——. *God-Birthing: Toward Sacredness, Personal Meaning, and Spiritual Nourishment*. Liguori, Mo.: Triumph Books, 1994.

Edinger, Edward F. *The Creation of Consciousness: Jung's Myth for Modern Man*. Toronto: Inner City Books, 1984.

——. *The Bible and the Psyche: Individuation Symbolism in the Old Testament*. Toronto: Inner City Books, 1986.

——. *The Christian Archetype: A Jungian Commentary on the Life of Christ*. Toronto: Inner City Books, 1987.

——. *Transformation of the God-Image: An Elucidation of Jung's* Answer to Job. Toronto: Inner City Books, 1992.

——. *The Aion Lectures: Exploring the Self in C. G. Jung's* Aion. Ed. Deborah A. Wesley. Toronto: Inner City Books, 1996.

——. *Archetype of the Apocalypse: A Jungian Study of the Book of Revelation*. Chicago: Open Court Publishing Company, 1999.

Eisler, Riane. *The Chalice and the Blade: Our History, Our Future*. New

York: HarperSanFrancisco, 1987.

Fox, Matthew. *Original Blessing: A Primer in Creation Spirituality.* Santa Fe, N.Mex.: Bear & Company, 1983.

————. *The Coming of the Cosmic Christ: The Healing of Mother Earth and the Birth of a Global Renaissance.* New York: Harper & Row, 1988.

Frye, Northrop. *The Great Code: The Bible and Literature.* Toronto: Academic Press Canada, 1982.

————. *Words With Power: Being a Second Study of The Bible and Literature.* Toronto: Penguin Books Canada Ltd., 1990.

Frymer-Kensky, Tikva. *In the Wake of the Goddesses: Women, Culture, and the Biblical Transformation of Pagan Myth.* New York: The Free Press, a Division of Macmillan, Inc., 1992.

Goswami, Amit, with Richard E. Reed and Maggie Goswami. *The Self-Aware Universe: How Consciousness Creates the Material World.* New York: G. P. Pitman's Sons, 1993.

Greene, Brian. *The Elegant Universe: Superstrings, Hidden Dimensions, and the Quest for the Ultimate Theory.* New York: W.W. Norton & Company, 1999.

Harpur, Tom. *Heaven and Hell.* Toronto: The Oxford University Press, 1983.

————. *The God Question: and Other Faith Issues.* Hansport, N.S.: Lancelot Press, 1993.

Hawking, Stephen. *A Brief History of Time: From the Big Bang to Black Holes.* New York: Bantam Doubleday Dell Publishing Group, Inc., 1988.

Hillman, James. *The Soul's Code: In Search of Character and Calling.* New York: Random House, 1996.

Hitchcock, John. *The Web of the Universe: Jung, the "New Physics" and Human Spirituality.* Mahwah, N.J.: The Paulist Press, 1991.

Hollis, James. *Tracking the Gods: The Place of Myth in Modern Life.* Toronto: Inner City Books, 1995.

————. *The Eden Project: In Search of the Mystical Other, A Jungian Perspective on Relationship.* Toronto: Inner City Books, 1998.

Hollyday, Joyce. *Clothed with the Sun: Biblical Women, Social Justice & Us.* Louisville, Ken.: Westminster/John Knox Press, 1994.

Houston, Jean. *The Possible Human: A Course in Enhancing Your Physical, Mental, and Creative Abilities.* Los Angeles: J. P. Tracher, Inc., 1982.

————. *The Search for the Beloved: Journeys in Sacred Psychology.* Los Angeles: Jeremy P. Tracher, Inc., 1987.

————. *The Hero and the Goddess: The Odyssey as Mystery and Initiation.* New York: Ballantine Books, 1992.

206

Johnson, Robert A. *Owning Your Shadow: Understanding the Dark Side of the Psyche.* New York: HarperSanFrancisco, 1991.

Jung, C. G. *Aion: Researches into the Phenomenology of the Self* (Bollingen Series XX). Trans. R. F. C. Hull, (Copyright 1959 by Bollingen Foundation). Fifth printing with corrections, Princeton, N.J.: Princeton University Press, 1959.

————. *Answer to Job* (Bollingen Series XX). Trans. R. F. C. Hull. (Copyright 1958 by Bollingen Foundation). Princeton, N.J.: Princeton University Press, 1973.

————. *Psychology and the East* (Bollingen Series XX). Trans. R. F. C. Hull. Princeton, N.J.: Princeton University Press, 1978.

————. *Psychology and Western Religion* (Bollingen Series XX). Trans. R. F. C. Hull. Princeton, N.J.: Princeton University Press, 1984.

————. *Memories, Dreams, Reflections.* Ed. Aniela Jaffé. New York: Random House. 1963. Vintage Books Edition, 1989.

Kaku, Michio. *Hyperspace: A Scientific Odyssey Through Parallel Universes, Time Warps, and the 10th Dimension.* New York: Oxford University Press, 1994.

Keen, Sam. *The Passionate Life: Stages of Loving.* New York: Harper & Row, 1983.

Levan, Christopher. *God Hates Religion: How the Gospels Condemn False Religious Practice.* Etobicoke, Ont.: The United Church Publishing House, 1995.

————. *Sin Boldly.* Etobicoke, Ont.: The United Church Publishing House, 1997.

Moore, Thomas. *The Care of the Soul: A Guide for Cultivating Depth and Sacredness in Everyday Life.* New York: Harper Collins, 1992.

Murray, Don. *For Unbelieving Christians: Rethinking the Christian Faith in Today's World.* Sackville, N.B.: Percheron Press, 1987.

Myss, Caroline. *Anatomy of the Spirit: The Seven Stages of Power and Healing.* New York: Three Rivers Press, 1996.

Parent, Mark. *Spirit Scapes: Mapping the Spiritual & Scientific Terrain at the Dawn of the New Millennium.* Kelowna, British Columbia: Northstone, 1998.

Rubenstein, Richard L. *The Cunning of History: Mass Death and the American Future.* New York: Harper & Row, 1975.

Sanford, John A. *The Kingdom Within: A Study of the Inner Meaning of Jesus' Sayings.* Philadelphia: J. P. Lippincott Company, 1970.

————. *The Man Who Wrestled With God: Light From the Old Testament on the Psychology of Individuation.* Mahwah, N.J.: Paulist Press, 1987.

————. *Mystical Christianity: A Psychological Commentary on the Gos-

pel of John. New York: The Crossroad Publishing Company, 1993.

Sheldrake, Rupert. *The Presence of the Past: Morphic Resonance and the Habits of Nature*. New York: Random House, 1988.

Spirit Mourn, Spirit Dance. Ed. Rebekah Chevalier. Etobicoke, Ont.: The United Church Publishing House, 1998.

Spong, John Shelby. *Born of a Woman*: *A Bishop Rethinks the Birth of Jesus*. New York: HarperSanFrancisco, 1992.

————. *Resurrection, Myth or Reality: A Bishop's Search for the Origins of Christianity*. New York: HarperSanFrancisco, 1994.

————. *Why Christianity Must Change or Die: A Bishop Speaks to Believers in Exile*. New York: HarperSanFrancisco, 1998.

Stein, Murray. *Jung's Map of the Soul: an Introduction*. Chicago: Open Court Publishing Company, 1998.

Tarnas, Richard. *The Passion of the Western Mind: Understanding the Ideas That Have Shaped Our World View*. New York: Ballantine Books, 1991.

Teilhard de Chardin, Pierre. *The Phenomenon of Man*. Trans. Bernard Wade. New York: Harper & Row, Harper Torchbooks, 1961.

The Five Gospels: The Search for the Authentic Words of Jesus. New Translation and Commentary by Robert W. Funk, Roy W. Hoover, and The Jesus Seminar. New York: HarperSanFrancisco, 1993.

The HarperCollins Study Bible: *New Revised Standard Version with the Apocryphal/Deuterocanonical Books*. General Ed. Wayne A. Meeks. New York: Harper Collins, 1993.

The New Oxford Annotated Bible With the Apocryphal/Deuterocanonical Books: An Ecumenical Study Bible: New Revised Standard Version. Eds. Bruce M. Metzger and Roland E. Murphy. New York: Oxford University Press, 1991.

The Other Bible: Ancient esoteric texts including Jewish Pseudepigrapha, Christian Apocrypha, Gnostic Scriptures, Kabbalah, Dead Sea Scrolls. Ed. Willis Barnstone. New York: HarperSanFrancisco, 1984.

von Franz, Marie-Louise. *C. G. Jung: His Myth in Our Time*. Trans. William H. Kennedy. (Originally published in 1975 by the C. G. Jung Foundation.) New York: G. P. Pitman's Sons, 1975.

Wilber, Ken. *No Boundary: Eastern and Western Approaches to Personal Growth*. Boston Mass.: Shambhala Publications, 1979.

————. *Up From Eden*. New York: Doubleday/Anchor, 1981.

————. *A Brief History of Everything*. Boston, Mass.: Shambhala Publications, 1996.

————. *Eye to Eye: The Quest for the New Paradigm*. 3rd ed. Boston, Mass.: Shambhala Publications, 1996.